KV-575-295

INTERNETWORKING LANs AND WANs
Concepts, Techniques and Methods

Internetworking is one of the fastest growing market in the field of computer communications. However, the interconnection of LANs and WANs ... conceptual and administrative difficulties. This ... enabling the reader to avoid the pitfalls

13 MAR 2001

THE MULTIPLEXER REFERENCE MANUAL

Designed to provide the reader with a detailed insight into the operation, utilization and networking of six distinct types of multiplexers, this book will appeal to practising electrical, electronic and communications engineers, students in electronics, network analysts and designers.
1993 0 471 93484 4

PRACTICAL NETWORK DESIGN TECHNIQUES

Many network design problems are addressed and solved in this informative volume. Gil Held confronts a range of issues including through-put problems, line facilities, economic trade-offs and multiplexers. Readers are also shown how to determine the numbers of ports, dial-in lines and channels to install on communications equipment in order to provide a defined level of service
1991 0 471 93007 5 (Book)
     0 471 92942 5 (Disk)
     0 471 92938 7 (Set)

NETWORK MANAGEMENT
Techniques, Tools and Systems

Techniques, tools and systems form the basis of network management. Exploring and evaluating these three key areas, this book shows the reader how to operate an effective network.
1992 0 471 92781 3

Please refer to the *tails*

PROTECTING LAN
RESOURCES

PROTECTING LAN RESOURCES
A COMPREHENSIVE GUIDE TO SECURING
PROTECTING AND REBUILDING A NETWORK

Gilbert Held
4-Degree Consulting
Macon, Georgia, USA

JOHN WILEY & SONS

Chichester · New York · Brisbane · Toronto · Singapore

Copyright © 1995 by John Wiley & Sons Ltd,
Baffins Lane, Chichester,
West Sussex PO19 1UD, England
National (01243) 779777
International (+44) 1243 779777

Reprinted November 1995

Other Wiley Editorial Offices

John Wiley & Sons, Inc., 605 Third Avenue,
New York, NY 10158–0012, USA

Jacaranda Wiley Ltd, 33 Park Road, Milton,
Queensland 4064, Australia

John Wiley & Sons (Canada) Ltd, 22 Worcester Road,
Rexdale, Ontario M9W 1L1, Canada

John Wiley & Sons (SEA) Pte Ltd, 37 Jalan Pemimpin #05–04,
Block B, Union Industrial Building, Singapore 2057

British Library Cataloging in Publication Data

A catalogue record for this book is available from the British Library

ISBN 0 471 95407 1

Typeset in 10½/12½ Bookman by Photo·graphics Ltd
Printed and bound in Great Britain by Redwood Books, Trowbridge, Wiltshire.

CONTENTS

PREFACE

The growth in the construction of local area networks truly represents the building boom of the 1990s with respect to the field of data communications. Organizations with hierarchical based mainframe networks have rapidly moved applications onto local area networks, while other organizations with existing LANs continue to expand their desktop computing and file-sharing capabilities. Accompanying this growth in the construction and utilization of local area networks is the realization that the LAN, like its predecessor the hierarchical mainframe based network, is subject to a variety of natural and man-created threats.

Unfortunately, many workstation users, network administrators and managers fail to recognize that the extension of the corporate network to the desktop can create a number of potential vulnerabilities that must be considered in addition to problems normally faced by conventional network users. While most organizations have the foresight to develop some type of disaster plan, that plan represents only a portion of the planning required to protect LAN resources. Recognizing this fact after being involved in the construction and operation of numerous local area networks resulted in a decision to prepare a comprehensive guide to protecting LAN resources.

The primary purpose of this book is to provide readers with a comprehensive guide to the numerous items that must be considered in securing, protecting and, if unfortunate circumstances warrant, rebuilding a network. To accomplish this, I have attempted to convey an insight into how certain LAN-related activities occur to illustrate various computer vulnerabilities as well as to indicate how to reduce such vulnerabilities. This will provide readers with a basic understanding of items to consider to secure and protect LAN resources.

Since the value of a network and its stored data varies from organization to organization, LAN vulnerabilities that may be of considerable concern to one organization may be a low-priority item or of little interest to other organizations. Recognizing this fact, my primary goal in writing this book was to provide information necessary to determine risk assessment and whether the cost associated with additional hardware or software is worth the benefit it provides. For example, in one chapter readers are presented with information concerning how to compute the availability levels of mirrored and disk duplexed systems. This information can be used to determine if the additional cost associated with obtaining one type of data storage system on a network file server over another type of storage system is warranted, based upon the different level of availability to data provided by each system.

As a professional author I truly welcome reader comments. You can write to me either directly or through my publisher whose address is on this book. Let me know if there is an area, topic or subject I have overlooked, or if you want an expansion of an existing topic; or feel free to send any other comments you may have. Many times, valuable reader comments have provided an insight to activities which work experience, travel and conference attendance fail to provide, and for this I am truly grateful.

Gilbert Held
Macon, Georgia

ACKNOWLEDGEMENTS

The publication of a book represents the culmination of a team effort I would be remiss if I did not acknowledge. As an old-fashioned author who travels extensively, I find it easier to take pen to paper than to use the modern convenience afforded by laptop computers, especially on long international flights where a search through previously written pages can be performed without fear of running out of battery power. Thus, I am grateful to Mrs Linda Hayes and Ms Junnie Heath for taking my long-hand manuscript—which includes the effect of writing when encountering air turbulence—and converting the results into a professional manuscript suitable for sending to my publisher.

Once again I am indebted to Ann-Marie Halligan for backing another one of my writing projects as well as for guiding the manuscript into the production process. Concerning the production process, I would like to thank Mr Robert Hambrook and his associates for their fine work which resulted in the book you are reading. Last but not least, I must thank my family for their understanding while I spent countless evenings and weekends working on this book.

1

BEYOND DISASTER RECOVERY

The protection of LAN resources represents a requirement to consider many factors beyond those associated with disaster recovery. Although the planning required to recover from different types of man-made and natural disasters is certainly important, it is also important to obtain an appreciation of the wide range of threats that can affect the operation of LANs, and countermeasures you can consider that may reduce or eliminate the necessity to perform a disaster recovery operation. Thus, the title of this chapter was selected to indicate the scope and direction of this book, which is oriented to the methods, procedures and policies you can consider to protect LAN resources, as well as the development of a disaster recovery plan you can put into effect should it become necessary.

In this chapter we will first focus our attention upon various components of a local area network and their individual and collective potential vulnerabilities. This will provide us with a detailed understanding of the problems we can face as a network user, administrator or manager, and why disaster recovery planning is only one element within the large number of elements you may wish to consider when developing a comprehensive plan to protect LAN resources. Using our knowledge of potential LAN vulnerabilities will provide a foundation for the review of network protection areas. This review will also serve as a reference to topics covered in detail in succeeding chapters.

1.1 LAN VULNERABILITY

To obtain an appreciation of the range of threats that can adversely effect the operation of a local area network, let us examine a schematic which illustrates the basic components associated with a LAN and its major points of vulnerability. Although Figure 1.1 illustrates a bus-based Ethernet network, the vulnerabilities shown are applicable to all types of LANs, to include Token-Ring and different types of IEEE 802.3 networks, such as 10BASE-T, which represent a hub-based version of Ethernet. Table 1.1 provides a brief description of each of the ten vulnerability areas shown in Figure 1.1.

Although most of the descriptions in Table 1.1 are self-explanatory, each area warrants a brief elaboration to indicate the relationship between network protection areas and threats which make local area networks vulnerable to the loss or modification of data, an inability of users to access network facilities and similar operation problems. In doing this we will obtain a tour of the focus of succeeding chapters in this book. However, prior to conducting that tour via an examination of network protection areas, let us obtain an appreciation of the threats we may face. By considering those threats we will be better prepared to plan for their occurrence as well as to develop appropriate contingency plans.

Network threats

Today it is difficult to pick up a newspaper or magazine without encountering an article that describes a potential or actual

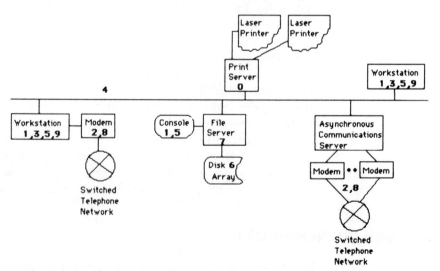

Figure 1.1   Common LAN vulnerability areas (see Table 1.1).

Table 1.1 Vulnerability areas illustrated in Figure 1.1.

Vulnerability area	Description
1	Unauthorized access to unattended but logged-in workstation or file server
2	Download of virus, work, time bomb or similar attack software
3	Transfer of attack software via diskette or boot from floppy to bypass controls
4	Monitoring of data flow on network media
5	Network access by observing entry of ID and password used by network user
6	Disk crash causes loss of data
7	Unauthorized access to sensitive files
8	Unauthorized transmission of sensitive data
9	Unauthorized duplication and removal of sensitive data on diskette
10	Inadvertent or intentional removal of another user's print job

threat to the operation of local and wide area networks. While acts of nature, such as the East Coast blizzard of 1994, the Los Angeles earthquake, Santa Monica mudslides, Midwest floods, Hurricanes Hugo, Andrew and Bob, and fires caused by lightning have been highly publicized, those incidents, while representing viable types of threats you must consider, only represent a fraction of the threats network facilities face.

Few persons go home in the evening worrying about the threat of a burst pipe, overflowing toilet, or stuck water fountain located on a floor above a network server. However, damage and destruction of network equipment due to internal building problems are much more prevalent than damage and destruction caused by acts of God.

Insurance companies normally do not issue policies to guard against the loss of data due to the inadvertent formatting of disks, their misplacement or destruction due to a slip of the wrist which spills a hand-held beverage onto a storage media, nor do they keep records of those types of data loss. If they did, such records would probably indicate that the "klutz" factor is a serious threat to network operations. While it is extremely difficult for a klutz to bring down a network, it is quite common for inadvertent operations to destroy months or years of work. Therefore, a knowledgeable, disgruntled employee as well as hackers and, for lack of a better word, other insidious persons who develop destructive software to include worms and viruses, represent another type of threat you must consider.

Threat categories

We can group potential network threats into five general categories. Those categories include acts of God and nature, building or environmental threats, unintentional human error, intentional human threats, and the failure of network components, the latter referred to collectively as hardware failures. Table 1.2 provides you with an indication of the variety of threats your network can face, grouped into the five categories.

In examining the threats listed in Table 1.2, it is relatively easy to shrug one's shoulders and say "it can't happen here". Hopefully the occurrence of those threats either on an individual or collective basis will not occur. However, it is important to recognize that not all threats have to represent the detonation of a bomb nor an act of God. A power glitch, coffee spill or disk crash can cause a considerable problem. While those threats do not warrant the implementation of a disaster recovery plan, administrative procedures and policies can significantly reduce the potential of those threats to adversely effect network operations. Similarly, policies and procedures as well as the use of filtering and scanning software may minimize the potential threat of malicious software. Thus, the old adage that "an ounce of prevention is worth a pound of cure" is especially applicable with respect to the protection of LAN resources.

1.2 NETWORK PROTECTION AREAS

The local area network vulnerability points illustrated in Figure 1.1 and described in Table 1.1 can be categorized into six general areas with respect to the use of tools, techniques and policies developed to protect network resources. By understanding the relationship between network vulnerability and network protection, we can develop realistic methods to protect LAN resources against different threats as well as develop a practical plan which can serve as a mechanism for the recovery of operations in the event of a disaster.

Table 1.2 Potential network threats.

Acts of god/nature

Earthquake	Insects
Flood	Lightning
Hail storm	Snow storm
Hurricane	Tornado
Ice storm	Wind storm

Building or environmental threats

A/C failure	Humidity
Brownout	Power outage
Burst pipe	Power spike
Communications carrier connection	Power surge
Condensation	Roof cave-in
Construction	Smoke damage
Coolant leak	Sprinkler discharge
Electrical fault	Static electricity
Fire	Toilet overflow
Frozen pipes	UPS failure

Unintentional human error

Cable cut	Software error
Erased data	Water/beverage spill
Program error	Incorrect print job routing

Intentional human error

Bomb threat	Theft
Bomb blast	Vandalism
Logic bomb	Virus
Sabotage	Worm
Terrorism	

Hardware failure

Disk drive failure	Print server failure
LAN adapter failure	Printer failure
Server failure	

Physical security

Physical security can be defined as the implementation of procedures which control access to computational facilities. Note that the physical access to different network components provides a mechanism to gain access to many LAN vulnerability areas, such as workstation diskette drives, file server consoles, and the output of network components. Later we will note the tradeoffs associated with providing different levels of physical access to network components, to include the effect of physical access barriers upon network user productivity.

Data security

There is a diminishing point of return with respect to implementing different levels of physical security. In all probability your network will include diskette drives and modems, and this means your network computers are vulnerable to different types of software attacks, including time bombs, worms, trojan programs, and viruses.

In Chapter 3 we will examine how attack software can affect the operation of network computers, and methods we can consider to prevent such attacks or recover from the effect of an attack which initially escaped detection. To provide readers with an understanding of the operations of attack software, as well as prevention and recovery methods, Chapter 3 has a detailed description of the structure of DOS disks, including key files which define how data is recorded on different types of media. Since most attack programs attempt to change a few key disk areas, this information explains why and how recovery becomes possible when it appears you cannot access information previously stored on your disks. It also explains how you can recover from human accidents, such as the inadvertent erasure of a critical file or the formatting of a disk by mistake.

Data storage protection

Disks are electromechanical devices that over a period of time can be expected to fail. The cause of failure can range in scope from unexpected vibration of equipment located near the drive, to power fluctuations. Thus, methods that can be used to extend the useful life of disks, provide a recovery mechanism when they fail, and enable operations to continue when a drive fails are important considerations which are the focus of Chapter 5.

In Chapter 5 we will examine the use of disk mirroring, disk duplexing and different types of redundant arrays of inexpensive disks, more commonly referred to as RAID levels, to obtain an appreciation of various methods that can be used to protect stored data. Using availability calculations presented in Chapter 4, we will also examine how we can compute the availability level of different disk subsystem configurations, which provides the tools necessary to perform a cost–benefit analysis. Since a stable power source is a key to protecting data, Chapter 5 also investigates the use of uninterruptable power supplies (UPS), including recently developed network-compliant UPS systems whose general characteristics can be viewed and modified via a local area network workstation.

Recognizing that the key to successful recovery from most disk failures is the backup of network data, Chapter 5 also discusses the use of backup equipment and techniques you can consider to minimize network disruptions due to a disk failure.

File access control

The unauthorized access to information stored on a network, either inadvertently or intentionally, represents another key LAN vulnerability area. In Chapter 6 we turn our attention to the tools and techniques we can use to control file access. We will examine file rights and permissions from both the workstation and file server perspectives.

Transmission security

In Figure 1.1 you will note that there are two vulnerable areas of a LAN with respect to communications. The transmission media which provide paths linking workstations and servers can be considered as the fabric which binds the network together. Any media failure can result in the inability of one or more workstations and servers to be accessible to other network users.

Although cabling problems are normally an infrequent occurrence and are rapidly resolved, occasionally the movement of machinery can result in the periodic generation of electrical magnetic interference (EMI) that can be difficult to locate. Another less frequent problem associated with the transmission media is that, with the exception of a few electronic mail programs, most communications between client and server are in the clear. This means that monitoring and recording of network activities by a technician trying to isolate a valid network problem, or by an unauthorized employee trying to obtain knowledge, can result in the disclosure of information that should normally be restricted.

The second area of network vulnerability with respect to communications concerns the transportation of information across carrier transmission facilities. Although only switched network communications via modems are illustrated in Figure 1.1, other areas of concern are the connection of LAN workstations to the Internet via the use of routers, and the use of leased lines to interconnect geographically separated LANs. Each of these activities results in a new series of potential threats which are discussed in Chapter 7.

Administrative security

Administrative security can be defined as the policies and procedures developed to minimize potential network vulnerabilities. In Chapter 8 we turn our attention to this area, examining the policies and procedures we can develop to minimize the effect of natural and man-made threats to the operation of our network. One of the key policies an organization should consider to minimize the effect of internal and external forces upon network operations is the development of a network bible, whose elements and placement are discussed in Chapter 8.

Contingency planning

There is a famous "Murphy's Law" which states that "whatever can go wrong will go wrong—at the worst possible moment". While we do not want to become a victim of that law, its potential threat is one of many things we must consider in developing contingency plans, which is the topic of the concluding chapter of this book.

PHYSICAL SECURITY AND ACCESS CONTROL

The term "physical security" is often associated only with cipher keylocks, guarded doors, controlled areas and the like, but these represent just one aspect of physical security. Another equally important aspect is the use of hardware and software which restrict the physical use of computers to authorized users. In this chapter we will focus upon both area access control and computer access control. However, prior to discussing physical security some general observations concerning security are warranted to provide readers with additional information concerning the protection of LAN resources.

In many dictionaries security is defined as "freedom from danger and risk". Although our concern in this chapter is physical security, readers should note that there are many other aspects of security that can minimize or reduce the potential for exposing LAN resources to adverse conditions. While just about all data centers include heat, smoke and water detection sensors to generate alarms when a threshold of temperature, number of airborne particles or humidity level is reached, many small organizations that have never operated a data center often fail to note the value of appropriate sensors until it is too late. One common problem is the tendency to rely upon building sensors which may become activated after a fire spreads from one area to another. While such sensors may generate alarms that save the building from destruction, their usefulness to save your organization's valuable data stored on tape or disk may not be effective.

In addition, it is important to review just what occurs when sensors become activated. For example, are sprinklers activated when smoke or heat sensors are activated? If so, do the sprinklers represent a new threat to your LAN resources that must be considered? Although the focus of this chapter is upon physical security and area access control, you must consider all potential threats to your LAN resources to develop and implement an effective plan. Thus, different types of sensors as well as the effect of activation of those sensors should be considered as keys to protecting your LAN resources.

2.1 AREA ACCESS CONTROL

Area access control, as its name implies, consists of methods and procedures used to control access to specific areas within an organization. Normally, the first line of protection is the building guard or floor receptionist, but other types of possible protection include cipher locks used to provide access to organizational work areas, conventional key locks to doors, and the use of visitor badges.

Although these methods usually provide a high degree of control, for persons outside the organization gaining access to areas where it is preferable they not access, there are other mechanisms you should consider when designing the layout of a LAN. These involve the location of workstations, file servers, print servers, hubs, and network cabling, and can be used to significantly reduce the potential for the inadvertent or intentional viewing, copying or modification of organizational data or changing the operational status of the network. Thus, let us discuss the placement of various network components with respect to access control prior to discussing methods that can restrict the use of computer equipment to authorized individuals.

Workstations

Regardless of whether a workstation is placed in an individual office or within a modular office work area, you can facilitate its physical security by making its use *observable*. This will make the use of the computer observable to persons walking by the office or workarea, making it more difficult for a person to access network facilities from a workstation logged onto the network while the authorized user is on a coffee break, attending a meeting or at lunch.

Although most network administrators ask users to logout of

the network when they leave their office or work area, typically many fail to do so. Then, it becomes a simple matter for a person walking by to use the existing connection without observation of their activity. In fact, this author knows of one practical joke in which a person walked by an executive's workstation, logged into the network E-mail system, and composed a short message concerning the relocation of the branch office to Philadelphia. By sending the message from the executive whose office he was in to another executive and, on purpose, carbon copying (ccing) the wrong distribution list to send, copies of the message were sent to a large number of employees and as a consequence the organization's productivity was disrupted for several days. In this situation the transmission of the fake message provided evidence of the illegal use of the workstation and served to underline the importance of logging off the network when employees leave their immediate work area. In other situations you may not be so fortunate, as a logged-in workstation normally enables access to data files for which the legitimate user has appropriate permissions. Within a few minutes an unauthorized employee can easily copy or modify data from important files, with most or all of the activity being undetected.

File servers

The hardware configuration of a file server is an important factor when determining its placement. If your file server uses removable storage, it is a good idea to place it in a restricted area behind a locked door. Otherwise, it becomes possible for an employee working late or even for a visitor to walk off with megabytes of corporate data.

Although some server operating systems require the console operator to be logged onto the system to "dismount" a mounted volume, some removable hardware can be made to automatically remove a mounted volume by simply powering off and then turning power back on to the device. Other servers may be connected to jukebox CD-ROM systems or disk arrays which also make it easy for a person to walk away with a large database. Thus, regardless of the type of password mechanism to protect access to a file server, it is a good idea to place the server either within a very observable area or in a room to which access can be physically controlled.

For situations where controlled access to work areas may not be possible, Lampertz (North America) Corporation of Peachtree City, GA, markets a series of Techno-Data®-Safes. Designed to secure equipment outside of normal controlled access areas, such as computer rooms, Techno-Data-Safes can be used to house file servers, print servers, hubs, and other types of network components within different sized steel enclosures.

The doors to the Techno-Data-Safes can be obtained with combination locks or card reader and electronic combination locks, similar to conventional safes. A special air intake/venting housing which provides air conditioning and filtration results in the Techno-Data-Safe being water resistant, fire proof, and able to withstand caustic gas. Thus, in addition to providing physical security to equipment whose access may not be controllable, you can also obtain protection against building disaster to equipment and data stored in a Techno-Data-Safe.

Although the Techno-Data-Safe and similar products provide a degree of security against the effect of a fire, it is important to remember that as the duration of a fire increases the temperature inside the safe will eventually increase, and at some point the stored media will become unusable. Thus, the use of any type of safe is no substitute for the creation of backup data and its placement at an offsite storage location, a topic discussed later in this book.

Print servers

Many network administrators overlook access control to print servers and printers attached to those servers. All too often the placement of a print server is considered solely with respect to the convenience of the user or user group.

In considering locations to place a print server you should first consider the type of material to be printed. If the printer will be used to produce sales reports, strategic plans and other documents that are not for general dissemination, you may wish to consider balancing the convenience of the location of the print server against the accessibility of its printed output to persons walking by the printer.

In some organizations print servers are located in access controlled areas along with file servers, while other organizations feel convenience of location of the server is of primary concern and do not consider the contents of printed documents to have any consequence if picked up by the wrong person. Thus, print server and network printer placement should be based upon the information content of material to be printed, the potential threat to the observation or removal of that material, and the convenience of users to access printed material.

Hubs

For Token-Ring and 10BASE-T networks, hubs are the terminating points of cabling to individual workstations, print servers and file servers. From a security perspective it is a good idea to locate hubs in a controlled access area since the inadvertent or intentional movement of cable can cause a network to fail. Another reason for locating hubs in a controlled access area is that many organizations connect test and diagnostic equipment to a port on the hub to monitor network activity. That monitoring can include the contents of frames being transmitted, which can be a significant reason to bar access to monitoring equipment to persons that have no reason to use such equipment.

In many organizations, hubs, test equipment, servers and communications circuits connected to a LAN are placed in a common controlled access location. Depending upon network activity, that location may also represent the office of the network administrator or network administration staff. Other times, in a large organization, a help desk area may include the previously described equipment.

When considering where to place equipment you must obviously examine the tradeoff between easy accessibility for administrators and users of network facilities and the different levels of security proviced by different types of controlled access. However, you should also consider the type of information transmitted on the network and the potential threat. For example, if your network is used for administrative activities and access to the building is controlled, you might prefer convenience of equipment location against controlled access to equipment. Conversely, if the LAN is used by the Bureau of Labor Statistics to compute CPI data which can affect the price of stocks and bonds and is released to the public several days after it is computed, you would more than likely want access to the LAN tightly controlled.

2.2 COMPUTER ACCESS CONTROL

Computer access control can be considered as the first line of protection to data resources once a person is physically able to access a computer. The earliest developed method of computer access control remains the primary method currently used, an association of a password to a user ID.

While an ID–password sequence is appropriate for many organizations, there are a number of potential problems, including a requirement to ensure users do not post passwords on consoles or provide their passwords to other users. Other problems include a tendency of persons to select easy-to-remember passwords, the administrative task involved in managing password changes on a regular basis, and the fact that an ID–password sequence, even when entered correctly, does not verify the authenticity of the person. Recognizing these problems, hardware and software developers have introduced a number of products that can be used to improve computer access control.

Software

Most network operating systems provide a basic level of password protection. To illustrate this let's examine the use of the NetWare SYSCON utility program by a network supervisor to control the use of passwords in a NetWare environment.

NetWare's SYSCON

Figure 2.1 illustrates the window labeled "Account Restrictions For User FRED" displayed in response to a NetWare user with supervisory rights first selecting "User Information" from the SYSCON utility program window, followed by selecting the username FRED from a list of usernames supported by the server and then selecting the "Account Restrictions" entry from a window labeled "User Information" which is displayed for the selected user. Note in Figure 2.1 that the field associated with the "Require Password" label was set to "No". This permits anyone with knowledge of the username FRED to login to the network and take full advantage of any rights associated with that user. Thus, one of the first items of business for a network administrator is to change the value of that field to "Yes". Doing so

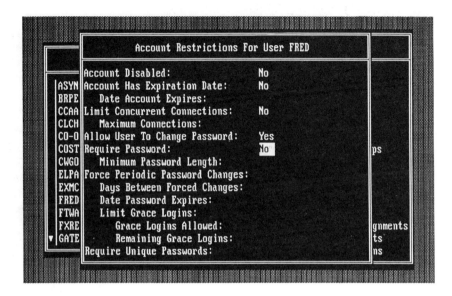

```
                    Account Restrictions For User FRED
      ┌────┐ Account Disabled:              No
      │ASYN│ Account Has Expiration Date:   No
      │BRPE│    Date Account Expires:
      │CCAA│ Limit Concurrent Connections:  No
      │CLCH│    Maximum Connections:
      │CO-O│ Allow User To Change Password: Yes
      │COST│ Require Password:              No               ps
      │CWGO│    Minimum Password Length:
      │ELPA│ Force Periodic Password Changes:
      │EXMC│    Days Between Forced Changes:
      │FRED│    Date Password Expires:
      │FTWA│ Limit Grace Logins:
      │FXRE│       Grace Logins Allowed:                     gnments
    ▼ │GATE│      Remaining Grace Logins:                    ts
      └────┘ Require Unique Passwords:                       ns
```

Figure 2.1 Examining password control field settings using the NetWare
SYSCON utility program.

results in the assignment of default values for the following
eight fields below the "Require Password" field.

Figure 2.2 illustrates the default values assigned to fields
which control password parameters. The value of the minimum
password length field must be between 1 and 20. If the "Force
Periodic Password Changes" field setting is left as "Yes" you can
then keep or modify the four fields following that field; otherwise
setting the field to "No" results in the elimination of the values
assigned to those fields from the display. The days between forced changes can be between 1 and 365, supporting daily
through annual password changes. Setting the field associated
with the label "Limit Grace Logins" to "No" blanks the two fields
following that field. When set to "Yes" the number of grace logins, a term used to reference how many times a user can login
with an expired password, must be between 1 and 200. That
value controls the value in the field associated with the label
"Remaining Grace Logins" field. Finally, the field associated with
the "Require Unique Passwords" label when set to "Yes" requires
users to use a different password when they change passwords.
However, NetWare only maintains a record of the last six pass-

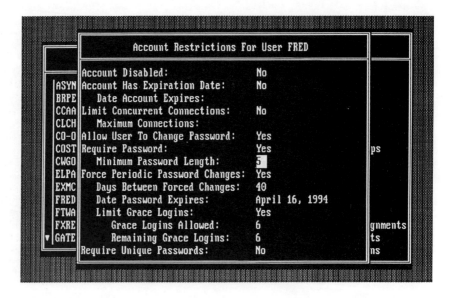

Figure 2.2 SYSCON utility program default settings for password protection.

words used, so a user can begin to repeat passwords in spite of the term used in the label for that field.

If the network supervisor or a person with supervisory rights simply wishes to change the password of a user, this can be accomplished by selecting the "Change Password" entry in the "User Information" window. This action results in the display of a window labeled "Enter New Password" as illustrated in Figure 2.3. As with most operating systems, NetWare will display the same window with the label "Retype New Password" to ensure it was entered correctly. If the field associated with the label "Allow User to Change Password" retains its default value of "Yes", any network user can use SYSCON to change their password through the use of SYSCON.

Password filtering and intruder detection and lockout

NetWare resembles most operating systems with respect to an inability to prevent the use of common names, reverse spelling of a user's full name, and other guessable entries that can result in the penetration of the network by a person who has access

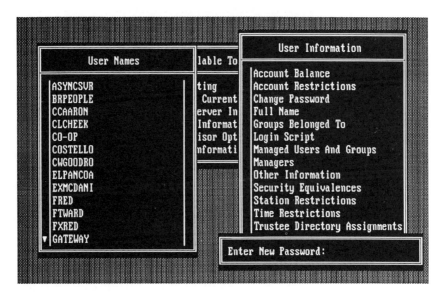

Figure 2.3 Using SYSCON to change a network user's password.

to a computer connected to the network. Owing to the lack of password entry filtering, several third party vendors introduced programs that add a degree of security by prohibiting the use of common and easily guessable passwords. Other products do that and more, working with the LAN operating system to restrict passwords to a minimum length while ensuring that the composition of the characters in the password is based upon the use of a pseudo-random number generator. Otherwise, passwords can be guessed, especially over a long weekend, by the construction and execution of a script program which cycles through all available password combinations.

Intruder detection and lockout To prevent successful trial-and-error guessing of a user's password, Novell's NetWare operating system includes an intruder detection lockout facility which a person with supervisory rights can enable via the use of the SYSCON utility program. The intruder detection and lockout option enables a person with supervisory rights to control the logging of attempts to access the network with invalid passwords. In addition, this facility can be used to prevent further attempts to login using a specific ID once a predefined threshold of user attempts is reached. Unfortunately, many sites running NetWare do not use this facility, although it is built into the network operating system. Thus, if you are the administrator of a NetWare network, be aware that enabling the intruder detection and lockout option will protect your network from penetration based upon a trial-and-error password entry attempt.

Password generation Another method you can use to ensure the integrity of passwords is to prevent the use of common terms, names, geographic locations, acronyms and other strings of characters that are susceptible to guessing. This is especially important if your network operating system does not support an intruder detection and lockout capability.

To facilitate the generation of passwords, third party software developers introduced a variety of products. One representative product is Password Genie™ from Baseline Software of Sausalito, CA. This program operates with NetWare and screens and generates passwords only when they are changed through the use of SYSCON and other NetWare utility programs. Password Genie permits users to select a password and then screens it against a 140 000 word American English dictionary as well as performing over 40 tests on the selection, ranging from acronym, geographic word, biographical word, and medical word comparisons, to a reversed user ID comparison. If the selected password passes Genie's tests it will be used. Otherwise, Password Genie provides a feedback tutorial concerning password generation to the user and enables the user to enter a revised password. The user is permitted a predefined number of attempts to enter a password based upon how the network administrator initiated the program. Once the user reaches the attempt threshold, Password Genie will assign a system generated password.

Hardware

Most computers currently manufactured are shipped with a built-in password protection capability. While this feature bars access to the computer from unauthorized users, its protection is easily overridden. For example, on some computers you can disable password protection by opening the system unit, disconnecting and then reconnecting the battery. Even if a built-in workstation's password protection feature was foolproof, which it isn't, once a user gains access to the computer's facilities and goes to lunch the computer typically remains powered-on and available for another person to use.

Recognizing the previously described problems associated with the manufacturer's password protection built into computer workstations, vendors introduced a variety of hardware and software products to secure network workstations as well as verify the authenticity of the person using the workstation. Some of those products are based upon the use of special adapter cards inserted into the system unit of the workstation, while others use password tokens generated by a special card similar in size to a conventional credit card and special semiconductors enclosed within a "steel button". These should not be confused with so called "data protection" locks which are low-cost molded plastic products with a built-in keylock designed to prevent access or use of a floppy drive, mouse, or keyboard. As with many PC tubular key locks, the keys for those products are about as hard to acquire as common luggage keys and their "protection" is easily overcome.

Adapter cards

An example of a hardware adapter card is StationLock™ from Trend Micro Devices of Torrance, CA. StationLock is a circuit board designed to fit into any Industry Standard Architecture (ISA) 8-bit expansion slot. This adapter card interacts with the computer's BIOS to have its ROM code activated prior to the operating system files being loaded, preventing the placement of a DOS diskette in drive A circumventing the system.

In addition to StationLock protecting access to the computer via password protection, this product can be used to protect access to floppy disks, COM ports, printer ports, and other ports of your workstation. This can be a very valuable feature, since it can allow other persons to use your computer without them having the capability to load or copy software. StationLock permits the granting of one of three access privileges for up to seven users and includes a rule-based virus trap. The latter feature monitors for the occurrence of virus-like activity.

Although anyone can override StationLock by removing the adapter from the workstation, this action does not necessarily result in a user obtaining access to the computer's hard disk. Since StationLock permits a valid user to encrypt the partition or boot record on the hard disk, the removal of the adapter card or its continued use without the proper password preclude the ability to use the hard disk.

Password tokens

One of the problems associated with most physical security methods is that, once overcome, the use of a file server console or conventional workstation can provide access to information that may be embarrassing or harmful if disclosed. An additional level of protection of data resources can be accomplished through the use of a remote authentication mechanism which is built into or supplements the physical security commonly associated with computers through the use of IDs and passwords. Currently the most popular type of remote authentication system is based upon a device which looks very similar to a pocket calculator but functions as a mechanism to generate and display a password token each time its owner logs onto a system.

The use of a token generator supplements or replaces the conventional use of user IDs and passwords.

Some token generators, such as the Security Dynamics (Cambridge, MA) SecurID™ card, generate a new password every 60 seconds and do not include any keys. A user simply views the passcode displayed in the card's LCD window and enters the passcode once they have logged into a server. The server prompts the user to enter their memorized Personal Identification Number (PIN), which verifies that the holder of the card is authorized to have the card in his or her possession.

Although this type of token generator provides a higher level of security than static passwords, which often are displayed on a user's terminal, care should be taken in issuing PIN numbers. Quite often the first or last n digits of a person's Social Security Number, numeric date of birth, or another simple to remember numeric sequence are used. This has resulted in several persons who left their token generator on their desk having an associate enter the network as a practical joke, since the method of assignment of PINs within the organization was well known.

Types of products

The SecurID token generator can be classified as a time-synchronized authentication system as it calculates a password every 60 seconds based upon a seed entered into the card and the current time. Two other types of token generators that warrant discussion are challenge–response and transaction-synchronized generators.

A challenge–response token generator is similar in size to a calculator but, unlike the SecurID card, includes a keypad. Figure 2.4 illustrates a typical device.

In a challenge–response authentication system, the host or server generates a pseudo-random number and transmits that number when a user attempts to access system resources. The user enters the received number into the token generator, which computes a response based upon an algorithm imbedded in the card. That response is transmitted by the user to the host which compares it with an expected value and provides access to system resources upon a match. Vendors that currently market challenge–response token generators include Enigma Logic Inc., Racal–Guardata, Digital Pathways Inc., and CrytpoCard Corporation.

The third type of token generator used to provide authentication is a transaction-synchronized device. This type requires the host and token generator to keep track of successful sign-ons since they use the last successful password to compute the next password. A transaction-synchronized token generator card contains a single button which is pressed to generate the next password. One of the problems associated with this type of token generator card is the fact that inadvertent pressing of

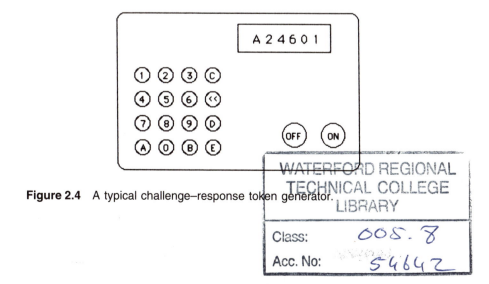

Figure 2.4   A typical challenge–response token generator.

the button results in a loss of synchronization between the token generator card and host.

Although token generators provide a solution to the authentication of users they are not foolproof. As with passwords associated with user IDs, they can be easily compromised by being left on a desk after use when a person goes to lunch or takes a break. However, since the authorized user is likely to note its disappearance and alert an appropriate person to eliminate its support, the potential exposure is typically less than with a conventional password.

Button protection

The evolution of microelectronic packaging and semiconductor technology resulted in the development of a new mechanism to protect LAN resources which, for want of a better term, is referred to as "button protection" because of the physical shape of the package. Developed by Dallas Semiconductor, and called MicroCan™ owing to the small size of the stainless steel enclosure which holds a special type of semiconductor, this device has been applied in a variety of identification situations, ranging from its use to prevent the theft of vehicles and as a mechanism to open a door lock, to its use with a computer to limit access to persons who have the correct button.

The key to the use of the MicroCan is a button reader which reads information stored in the button. Several types of button readers have been developed, including one built into a keyboard and a probe type device which can be cabled to a computer's serial port.

Dallas Semiconductor markets the MicroCan with button readers and software as a mechanism which allows a network administrator to grant or deny access to files on a network by distributing buttons and passwords protecting their contents. Dallas Semiconductor provides software, marketed under the name Dallas SignOn™, which is loaded onto a LAN server; this enables the network administrator to program passwords into buttons through the attachment of a button reader to the server. This software also enables the network administrator to select files to be protected by associating a 64-bit ID programmed into each button to specific files.

Each client workstation to be used with a MicroCan is retrofitted with button readers that are built into a special keyboard or connected to the serial port of the computer. Buttons are distributed to appropriate users to connect to badges or key rings. Then, instead of typing a password upon logon, the user is prompted to touch their button to a button reader. The server software compares the information read from the button to data previously entered in the server to provide general access to the network as well as specific access to files.

At the time this book was prepared the Dallas SignOn software was compatible with NetWare 3.X and 4.0 based LANs. However, by the time you read this book the software should also work with Windows NT, VINES, and LAN Server based networks. The firm markets two different configurations of its SignOn product, referred to as S-Paks for servers and C-Paks for clients. The S-Pak contains a button reader and software to protect files and construct a repository of button information. The C-Pak contains a button and a button reader. If a button is lost or stolen the user would report its loss to the network administrator who would update the database. Then, if someone attempted to use that button after the database was updated, software in the server would cause the lost or stolen button to self-destruct by writing over all previously recorded information, thus making the button useless.

3

DATA SECURITY

In this chapter we turn our attention to data security, a term used by this author to denote the prevention of or recovery from intentional or unintentional alteration of data. Although many articles and books whose topics cover data security are primarily focused upon viruses, in actuality, while important to consider, a virus represents one of many causes of data corruption.

The primary cause of data corruption is the eventual failure of the disk drives used on a network. As an electromechanical device a disk drive is subject to both electrical and mechanical failure. Its read/write head mechanism can fail, vibration can adversely effect read/write head movements, or a power failure or power surge can cause havoc with a data read or write operation. While you can use an uninterruptible power supply (UPS) to eliminate the effect of power variations on disk performance, as discussed in Chapter 5, doing so simply prolongs the life of the disk but does not eliminate the fact that it will eventually fail. Thus, the best methods to compensate for the eventual failure of a disk drive are first to perform regular backup operations, and second to consider the use of different types of redundant arrays of inexpensive disks (RAID) systems, disk duplexing, or disk mirroring, topics discussed also in Chapter 5. Each of these methods is based upon the use of different types of hardware whose utilization adds a level of redundancy to protect data previously stored.

Since Chapter 5 covers methods to protect stored data from disk failures, we will turn our attention here to software attacks that can cause harm to individual workstations or to all computers connected to a network.

We shall first review how data is stored on a disk and how the computer operates when it is powered up or a system reset is performed. This information will enable us to recognize the effects of different types of software attacks upon computer operations and methods we can use to protect our computer equipment from those attacks or recover from the effect of attacks we did not prevent.

3.1 DISK STORAGE

Data is stored on disks on concentric circles referred to as "tracks", as illustrated in Figure 3.1.

Diskettes

On a $3\frac{1}{2}$-inch diskette there are 80 tracks, numbered from 0 at the outer edge to 79 on the inner part of the disk. On a double-sided disk information can be stored on each side. The top side of the disk is known as side 0, while the bottom is referred to as side 1. The pair of tracks that lie over each other are collectively referred to as a "cylinder". Thus, you can refer to both track 0, side 0 and track 0, side 1 together as "cylinder 0".

Depending on the diskette used, the type of drive used to format the diskette, and the PC user's FORMAT command specification, each track is subdivided into either 8, 9 or 18 sectors, with each sector having space to store 512 eight-bit bytes of information. For a diskette formatted for 18 sectors per track, its storage capacity becomes 2 sides times 80 tracks per side

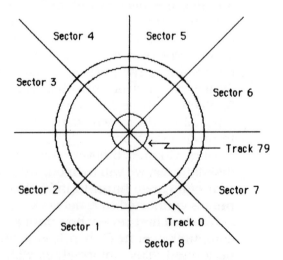

Figure 3.1   Disk track and sector relationships on a $3\frac{1}{2}$-inch diskette.

times 18 sectors per side times 512 bytes per sector, yielding 1 474 560 bytes (1.44M bytes) of data storage.

Hard disks

Hard disks have a similar relationship between tracks and sectors as diskettes. However, their higher rotational speed and the use of a rigid surface permits the hard disk to hold more tracks per side and sectors per track. Another significant difference between diskettes and hard disks concerns the use of multiple platters in many hard disks. When two or more platters are used in a hard disk, the scheme used for numbering each side of each platter can be likened to numbering each side of a single platter drive. That is, the top of the first platter is still referred to as side 0 and its bottom is known as side 1. The top of the second platter becomes side 2, while the bottom of the second platter becomes side 3, and so on. Collectively, all of the sides of all platters for track n are referred to as cylinder n.

Formatting and addressing

Information stored on a disk must be retrievable to be useful. Thus, a mechanism is required to identify the location where data is stored so that it can be retrieved. That mechanism is obtained by placing an identifying mark or *address* on each sector, a process which occurs when a disk is formatted.

There are two types of formatting that can occur, depending upon the type of storage media used—physical formatting and logical formatting.

Physical formatting

Physical formatting involves writing the address of each sector into the sector as a header or preamble to the location where sector data will be stored. The process also adds synchronization and gap bytes. Synchronization bytes prefix the header and "wake up" the controller to the fact that it is about to read a sector address, whereas gap bytes can be considered as filler bytes placed between sectors which enable the controller to obtain a degree of timing tolerance between having to read information stored across multiple sectors.

Logical formatting

Under logical formatting the operating system organizes the disk into directories and creates an index area which will contain pointers to locations where files will be stored on the disk. Hard disks are supplied with physical or low-level formatting already performed on the media, so use of the FORMAT command skips the physical formatting process and results in logical formatting. In comparison, when you format a diskette the FORMAT command performs a physical format followed by a logical format.

Disk areas

Under DOS, both diskettes and hard disks are organized into four main areas when a logical format occurs. Those areas are the boot sector, File Allocation Table (FAT), root directory and data area. On a hard disk that can be partitioned into two or more areas to support different operating systems, the disk will include a fifth area referred to as a Partition Table, which includes a revised boot sector as part of the Partition Table.

Boot sector

The boot sector is a short program which occupies the first sector of the first track of the top side of a disk—sector 1, track 0, side 0. When a computer is powered on or a system reset operation is performed, an attempt is first made to read drive A. If there is no disk in drive A the computer then attempts to read drive C. What is actually happening is that logic in the computer causes it to first search for a disk in drive A and, if found, read the boot sector.

The boot sector contains a short program which loads the rest of the operating system as well as information concerning how data is stored on the disk. The program which loads the remainder of the operating system loads two hidden files, one which loads the Basic Input/Output System (BIOS) and a second file which contains the Disk Operating System (DOS). On a PC-DOS system the two hidden fields are typically named IBMBIOS.COM and IBMDOS.COM and may be named differently on non-IBM personal computers. If you do not have a system disk in drive A, the boot sector program will display the message "non-system disk, replace and hit any key". If you do not have any disk in drive A the computer will then attempt to read the boot sector of your hard disk.

Concerning data storage, the boot record includes information which indicates the physical characteristics of the disk and its logical storage of data. Items included in the boot record are the number of bytes per sector, number of tracks, number of sectors per track, and the number of platters. Thus, the boot sector contains critical information which governs the ability of the computer both to load the operating system as well as to recognize data stored on the disk.

File Allocation Table

The File Allocation Table (FAT) records the status of storage units on a disk. On a diskette the FAT records the status of sectors, whereas on a hard disk the status of clusters which represent a grouping of logically consecutive sectors are recorded. In actuality, on a diskette a cluster represents one sector, so we can say that the FAT records the status of clusters on both diskettes and hard disks, although the number of sectors per cluster will vary depending upon the type of disk used.

Under DOS 2.X, FAT entries are 12 bits in length, permitting 4096 unique entries. If each number denotes a 512-byte sector, the maximum capacity of the disk becomes 4096 times 512 or 2 097 152 bytes. To increase available storage, DOS 2.X assigns each FAT entry to a cluster of 8 logically consecutive sectors on a hard drive, expanding total recognizable storage to 4096 times 4096 or 16 777 216 bytes. Under DOS 3.X and later versions of that operating system, the FAT was changed so each entry could be either 12 or 16 bits in length. When a 2-byte number is used the largest sector number becomes 65 536. Since DOS sector numbering commences with 0 and each sector can hold 512 bytes, the maximum number of addressable bytes becomes 65 536 times 512 or 32M bytes. To permit addressing beyond 32M bytes, DOS 4.0 and later versions of that operating system expanded the number of bytes used to specify a sector to 4, permitting up to 4 billion sectors to be addressed.

Table 3.1 Possible FAT entries.

Hex value	Meaning
0000	Available cluster
0002-FFEF	Cluster used for file storage. Entry points to next cluster used by file
FFF0-FFF6	Reserved for future use
FFF7	Bad cluster
FFF8-FFFF	Last cluster in a file

Actual entries in the FAT indicate whether a cluster is available for use, used by a file, or defective. During the logical formatting process DOS writes addressing information for each sector. It follows that information by placing a special byte (hex F6) in each sector data area and attempts to read previously written information. Clusters that contain one or more sectors that cannot be properly read are identified in the FAT as bad clusters by the entry FFF7. Table 3.1 lists the four possible values each FAT entry can have.

The actual cluster numbering in the FAT commences with 2 and represents a group of sectors whose number is based upon the version of DOS used. The first two entries in the FAT are reserved for special information, while the third entry holds information about the first cluster, which under DOS is numbered cluster 2. The next entry holds information about the second cluster, numbered cluster 3, and so on.

The root directory

The root directory can be considered as the third part of system information stored on a disk. Directly following the FAT, the root directory's size is based upon the type of disk used. On a hard disk the root directory can hold up to 512 entries of 32 bytes that can reference either subdirectories or files. Table 3.2 lists the fields associated with each directory entry.

Filename codes

As with FAT entries, DOS uses special codes to indicate the status of the filename field. A 0 in the first byte of a filename

Table 3.2 Directory entry fields.

Field	Size (bytes)
Filename	8
Extension	3
Attributes	1
Reserved	10
Time	2
Date	2
Starting FAT entry	2
File size	4

indicates an unused directory entry. This provides DOS with the ability to recognize that it has reached the end of active directory entries without having to search through all entries in the directory.

A period (.) as the first byte of the filename is used by DOS for navigation around the directory structure and references the current directory.

The third filename code is hex E5, which is placed in the filename field to indicate that a file was erased. This explains why disk "unerase" programs as well as the DOS UNDELETE command can recover erased files but lose the first character in the name of a recovered file. If you should inadvertently erase a file it is important that you do not perform any file-saving operation until you recover the deleted file. The reason for this is that once a file is erased and DOS places the filename code hex E in the filename field, the sectors previously used by the erased file become available for use.

Beginning with DOS 5.0, Microsoft licensed several utility programs from Central Point Software for inclusion in their disk operating system. Two of the more popular programs are UNDELETE and MIRROR which are now included in DOS as commands.

Figure 3.2 illustrates the help screen generated by DOS for the UNDELETE command, while Figure 3.3 illustrates the help screen for the MIRROR command. Each help screen indicates the function performed by the command, its format or syntax and the use of optional parameters supported by the command.

To illustrate the use of UNDELETE, let us delete a file. Figure 3.4 illustrates deletion of the file NORTN1.PZI followed by use of the UNDELETE command with the /LIST option. Note that

```
C:\PZP)help undelete
Restores files which have been deleted.

UNDELETE [[drive:] [path]] [filename] [/LIST | /ALL] [/DT | /DOS]

    /LIST    Lists the deleted files available to be recovered.
    /ALL     Undeletes all specified files without prompting.
    /DT      Uses only the deletion-tracking file.
    /DOS     Uses only the MS-DOS directory.

MIRROR, UNDELETE, and UNFORMAT Copyright (C) 1987-1991 Central
Point Software, Inc.
```

Figure 3.2   DOS UNDELETE command help screen.

```
C:\PZP)help mirror

Records information about one or more disks.

MIRROR [drive:[ . . .]] [/1] [/Tdrive[-entries] [ . . .]]
MIRROR [/U]
MIRROR [/PARTN]

  drive:     Specifies the drive for which you want to save information.
  /1         Saves only the latest disk information (does not back up previous
             information).
  /Tdrive    Loads the deletion-tracking program for the specified drive.
  -entries   Specifies maximum number of entries in the deletion-tracking file.
  /U         Unloads the deletion-tracking program.
  /PARTN     Saves hard disk partition information to a floppy diskette.

MIRROR, UNDELETE, and UNFORMAT Copyright (C) 1987-1991 Central Point Software,
Inc.
```

Figure 3.3   DOS MIRROR command help screen.

the command shows the filename as ?ORTN1.PZI since erasure
of the file resulted in replacement of its first letter by hex E.
   In Figure 3.3 note the /PARTN option. This option saves your
hard disk partition to a diskette and its use can be quite valuable if your computer ever becomes infected by a virus that
attacks your boot partition, a frequent method of attack used
by virus developers and described later in this chapter. Thus,
MIRROR provides you with a valuable weapon to counteract the
adverse effect of many types of viruses.

```
C:\PZP)erase nortn1.pzi

C:\PZP)undelete /list

Directory: C:\PZP
File Specifications: *.*

        Deletion-tracking file not found.

        MS-DOS directory contains 1 deleted files.
        Of those, 1 files may be recovered.

Using the MS-DOS directory.

        ?ORTN1 PZI 24849 2-19-94 11:43a . . .A
```

Figure 3.4 Using UNDELETE with the /LIST option.

3.2 POWER-ON OPERATION

Now that we have reviewed the structure of a disk and how the boot sector reads data, we examine in more detail what actually happens when you power-on your computer or perform a system reset operation. This sequence of events will be used in our discussion of software attacks to better understand methods we can use to recover from an attack if our preventive measures fail.

POST

When you turn on power to your computer, instructions in Read Only Memory (ROM) are executed which test various components, including RAM memory. This test, in which each block of locations of RAM being tested is displayed, is referred to as the Power-On Self-Test (POST). POST always occurs when power is turned on but is bypassed when a system reset operation occurs.

Boot sector and system file loading

Once POST is completed or bypassed, additional code in ROM searches drive A for a system disk and will load the boot sector from the disk. If no disk is in drive A, ROM then searches the hard drive for a boot sector. Once a boot sector is located in either drive A or drive C, the program on the boot sector is loaded into memory. That program defines the disk parameters, in effect telling the computer how data is recorded on the media. Then the program transfers control to two hidden files. Those files, commonly named IBMBIOS.COM and IBMDOS.COM, are placed on the disk when it is formatted using the /S option which places the operating system on the disk.

Since the boot sector informs the computer how data is recorded on the media, it knows how many sectors are contained in a cluster and the number of sides per cylinder.

To locate a file, such as IBMBIOS.COM, the root directory is searched for the appropriate filename entry. The only difference between this search and other file searches is that the system is searching for the hidden file with the name IBMBIOS.SYS, which means it checks the appropriate attribute byte bit position which denotes that the file is hidden once it locates the appropriate filename. After the appropriate directory entry is located, the 2-byte pointer to the starting entry of the file in the FAT is retrieved. That pointer is the address of the first cluster where the program is stored. If the file requires more than one cluster of storage the FAT entry, as indicated in Table 3.1, contains a value between hex 0002 and FFEF which points to the next cluster used by the file.

Once the second hidden file is loaded the computer looks for a special file named CONFIG.SYS which, as its name implies, contains configuration statements, including statements which, when processed, load device drivers that enable different types of hardware to be used with your computer. If CONFIG.SYS is found the statements in that file are executed.

Once this is accomplished, control is passed to a third operating system file called COMMAND.COM. Unlike the other two operating system files, COMMAND.COM is not a hidden file. This file is the command processor which interprets DOS commands you enter from the keyboard. Some commands, such as DIR for a directory listing, are known as "internal commands" as the actual code which performs the requested operation is included in COMMAND.COM. Other commands, such as FORMAT, are "external commands" and the code resides on a separate file which COMMAND.COM loads when you enter an external command.

As the final step in the power-on process, COMMAND.COM searches for the existence of a file named AUTOEXEC.BAT which, if found, is loaded and executed. AUTOEXEC.BAT contains any batch statements you placed in file to automate operations upon powering on your computer. Figure 3.5 summarizes the operations performed by a PC-DOS computer during its power-on cycle.

3.3 SOFTWARE ATTACK METHODS

Understanding how we can attempt to prevent different types of software attacks requires knowledge of the general types of programs unscrupulous persons have intentionally developed to cause harm to computers. The major categories of software that can harm computers include logic bombs, worms, trojans and viruses.

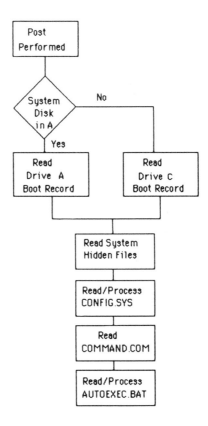

Figure 3.5 PC-DOS power-on operations.

Logic bombs

A logic bomb is a program which lies dormant until it is triggered by a specific event. The trigger can range in scope from a specific date or time to the execution of a valid program. Once activated the logic bomb will normally perform some type of insidious operation, such as changing the value of data previously stored on disk or altering the value of a RAM memory location.

Worms

A worm is a program which reproduces itself. Unlike a virus which both adversely infects and reproduces, the worm is relatively benign as it does not alter nor destroy data. However, each copy of the worm creates additional copies, which can rapidly use all available computer resources.

Worms are usually planted on networks and in multi-processing operating systems where they can do the most harm. In fact, the often referenced Internet virus which brought several thousand computers connected to that network to a halt was actually a worm.

Trojans

A trojan represents a program which functions as a delivery vehicle for destructive code which will adversely effect the operation of a computer. Named after the Trojan horse which hid soldiers, a trojan program will appear useful but when executed can function as a logic bomb, worm or virus.

Viruses

A virus is a program which reproduces its own code, placing its code in other programs so that when those programs are executed the infection spreads. The actual effect caused by a virus can vary from humorous to catastrophic. Some viruses may simply display the message "X Shopping Days till XMAS", while other viruses can alter your hard drive's boot sector, resulting in the apparent inability to access information pre-viously stored on your hard drive.

One of the most popular methods used by virus developers to replicate their code is to rename the program as an external DOS command file with the extension .COM when the real pro-gram has the extension .EXE. The reason for doing so is that when you enter a DOS command and the operating system encounters both .COM and .EXE files with the same filename, DOS will execute the file with the extension .COM. A smartly constructed virus using the .COM extension will also execute the DOS command as it spreads, hiding the effect of the infec-tion for a period of time until the cumulative effect of the virus replications becomes noticeable. This type of virus is commonly referred to as a .COM infector.

Types of viruses

The types of viruses you can encounter depend upon the ingen-uity of the hackers and pranksters that typically develop these programs. Although the types of viruses are virtually unlimited, they can be categorized by the most common areas they attempt to infect. Those areas are the boot sector and FAT, system files, and DOS commands.

Boot and FAT infectors A virus can cause a considerable amount of harm by changing information in the boot sector and/or file allocation table. By changing information in the boot sector a virus can make your hard disk appear to be unusable. By changing data in the FAT a virus can make portions of your disk "disappear" simply by marking good sectors as bad or changing a pointer to the next cluster used by a file to an end-of-file cluster value. A few viruses have been known to swap the starting FAT entry addresses in the root directory, which when done with database files can result in the subsequent execution of a database processing program using an output file as an input file and vice versa, a truly insidious trick!

System file infectors A system file virus infector to be truly hidden requires more knowledge and effort to develop than a virus which alters the boot sector, FAT or a directory entry value. For this reason, system file infectors are not commonly encountered, but their effect can be serious.

A system file infector changes one of the system files, such as IBMBIOS.COM, IBMDOS.COM, or COMMAND.COM. Since these files are always executed upon power-on, their modification functions as an easy mechanism to replicate a virus. Most virus developers simply attach their program code to a system file, so a virus scanner can easily note the occurrence of this type of file by noting an abnormal system file size. Far more difficult to detect is the virus which rearranges system file code so it can insert itself into the file without altering the size of the file. Fortunately, very few persons have the knowledge and are willing to devote the time required to develop this type of virus.

DOS command infectors A DOS command infector virus either attaches itself to an external DOS command file or hides itself by naming itself after an .EXE file using the extension .COM. Since DOS commands are frequently executed, a command infector achieves the ability to frequently replicate itself by pretending to be a DOS command.

Potential effects

Although a considerable amount of literature has been written about the potential effects of viruses, many people are disbelievers until they are personally adversely affected.

Figure 3.6 reproduces a letter issued by the Office of Personnel Management, a United States Federal Government Agency, to illustrate the effect of a virus brought into that agency by an unsuspecting and good intentioned employee who wanted to demonstrate the use of a graphics program to colleagues. This action wound up disrupting computer operations for several days.

Now that we have a basic knowledge of the types of software attacks we can encounter and the manner in which most viruses designed to cause harm operate, let's focus our attention upon methods we can consider to prevent a software attack and, if unsuccessful in our prevention methods, recover from the effect of an attack.

Office of Personnel Management   OPM EL No. A-755

Employee Letter

_____

                                                         Washington, DC 20415
                                                         October 30, 1990
SUBJECT:

     Computer Viruses

Several weeks ago, an agency personal computer system was inadvertently
damaged by the installation of unauthorized software that was infected with a
computer virus.

A virus is a hidden program that performs harmful operations deliberately
designed to corrupt computer programs, destroy data, or confound and irritate
microcomputer users. Most viruses are designed to replicate themselves once
they enter a computer or network. They usually attach themselves when someone
tries out a copy of an infected program.

The recent problem occurred when an OPM employee brought a computer graphics
demonstration program to the office and installed it on his computer system.
Unknown to this employee, a computer virus existed in this software. The
virus was not discovered until it had infected an OPM Local Area Network, and
the microcomputers of several OPM employees who unsuspectingly used the
software at their local work stations.

What started out as an innocent demonstration of computer graphics capabilities unfortunately disrupted operations for several days. Technicians and
other computer experts had to track down the infected computers, isolate the
software, remove it, and restore copies of authorized software for use on the
LAN and on individual microcomputers. The result was a considerable cost in
lost productivity and service to OPM's clients.

Unauthorized computer software is contrary to OPM policy as stated in the OPM
Administrative Manual, Chapter 57. OPM policy is to use Government purchased
software obtained from reputable sources. Other legitimate software may be
authorized, depending on the circumstances, but may never be installed on an
OPM computer without the specific authorization of your organization's
management. No other software is to be installed or used on an OPM computer
or network.

Many OPM groups and offices have an organization, or an individual, who acts
as the organization's clearinghouse on microcomputer matters. If you have
questions and concerns about viruses and their prevention, direct them to that
individual.

Supervisors and employees alike share in the responsibility to protect OPM's
microcomputers. Please protect yourself and OPM by using only authorized
software.

James B. Lancaster, Jr.
Associate Director
for Administration

Figure 3.6 Office of Personnel Management employee letter concerning
computer viruses.

3.4 DESTRUCTIVE SOFTWARE SOURCES

There are only two ways in which a virus can enter a computer— via a diskette or by communications. This means that an organization can implement a set of policies that can significantly reduce the possibility of a software attack occurring.

Entry via a diskette

The use of a diskette to distribute different types of destructive programs is well known. This is typically counteracted by an organization having a policy which precludes persons from bringing disks from home into the office.

What is not so commonly known is that even legitimate shrink-wrapped software may contain a virus. In fact, several cases have been documented where persons bought commercial software and, after altering one or more diskettes, returned the software to a computer store where the proprietor rewrapped the product in plastic and sold it. Other cases have been documented where a virus was added to a master diskette used to create thousands of copies of a commercial program which were shipped to mail order resellers and computer stores throughout the world.

Thus, while policies preventing employees from bringing unauthorized diskettes from home into the office may reduce the potential for infection via diskette, this does not represent a total elimination of the threat.

Entry via communications

Another common policy implemented by many organizations precludes the downloading of files from bulletin board systems. The rationale for this policy is that it is relatively easy to establish an account on most bulletin board systems under any name you care to use and upload a file which when downloaded by an unsuspecting party provides an unintended surprise. Recognizing this problem, many bulletin board system operators scan all uploaded files with virus detection software prior to making the files available for downloading by other BBS subscribers. Although this action does not completely preclude the possibility of destructive code being incorporated into a file, it significantly reduces the possibility that the file is infected.

A corporate policy precluding access to bulletin board systems can be expected to stop many persons from communicating with a BBS. However, someone may eventually download a program which contains code that adversely affects his or her computer. If that computer is connected to a network, within a short period hundreds of computers may become affected. If the computer is not connected to a network then the only way the infection can spread is via diskette when one user shares data or programs with another computer user.

Another method that has been used to attack computer users is through the inclusion of ANSI codes embedded within a file or even an electronic mail message. Although the use of ANSI codes will not result in the formation of an executable program, this strategy can be used to change the value assigned to a computer key. All of a sudden, pressing the F2 key, for example, might result in the generation of the DOS command ERASE *.DAT.

Since it is highly unlikely that you can totally eliminate the potential for harmful software to access your computer, it is important to understand techniques you can use to identify inappropriate software, recognize a software attack if the identification process fails, and methods you can use to recover from an attack.

3.5 INFECTION DETECTION AND PREVENTION

According to an article published in a national magazine during 1994, almost 4000 types of worms, bombs and viruses had been detected. This means that it is highly probable that no one prevention and detection strategy can be expected to represent an absolute guarantee against infection. However, such programs do represent a good starting point to protect your computer.

Infection prevention

Infection prevention software functions as a filter, examining computer operations susceptible to modification by different types of attack software. Most infection prevention software monitors all I/O operations and disallows any attempt by code to modify critical disk areas, such as the boot sector, FAT and executable files.

Typically, you load the infection prevention software on your hard disk and modify your AUTOEXEC.BAT file to load that program each time you use your computer. Then, the infection prevention program functions as a barrier to most of the commonly used attack software techniques known to result in destructive operations.

Since infection prevention software is designed to detect attack software once it begins to operate, such methods are normally used to locate dormant infections. To identify previously stored attack software requires the use of detection software.

Detection programs

A detection program, sometimes referred to as a virus scanner, searches your disk looking for identifying attributes associated with different types of attack software. Such software may examine the names of files to determine if any are disguised as DOS .COM files, look for replication code and search system files looking for any suspicious alterations.

One of the most popular anti-virus software products is now built into Microsoft Corporation's Windows. Although it is referred to as Microsoft Anti-Virus, if you select the Help menu bar and click on the "About Anti-Virus" entry you will note that Central Point Software was the developer of this program and holds its copyright.

You can access the Microsoft Anti-Virus for Windows program from the Windows Program Manager (Microsoft Tools) window. Anti-Virus is one of three tools built into Windows 3.1 as illustrated in Figure 3.7. By double-clicking on the Anti-Virus icon you can initiate the Anti-Virus detection program.

Figure 3.8 illustrates the Microsoft Anti-Virus window after the author double-clicked on his hard disk (drive C) icon. Doing so causes the program to read the directories in the selected

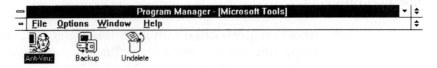

Figure 3.7 Anti-Virus is one of three tools built into Windows 3.1.

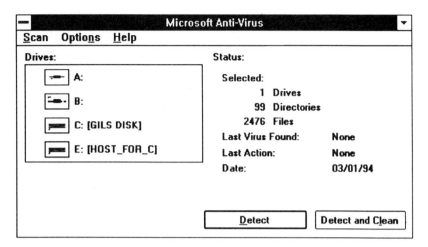

Figure 3.8 Microsoft Anti-Virus window displaying a summary of the directories and files on drive C after the author double-clicked on the icon for that drive.

drive and tabulate a running total of directories and files in the directories. This information provides an indirect indication of the amount of time that will be required if you select the "Detect" or the "Detect and Clean" button, since the time required to scan all of the files on a drive is proportional to the number of files on the drive.

Besides the "Detect" and "Detect and Clean" options the Anti-Virus program provides users with several additional options that are selected by clicking on the "Scan" menu. Figure 3.9

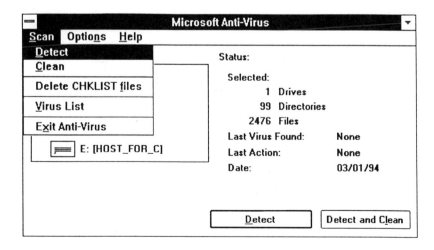

Figure 3.9 Microsoft Anti-Virus Scan menu.

illustrates the options in the Scan menu. Note that the "Clean"
option actually represents a "detect and clean" operation. Selecting the "Delete CHKLIST files" entry causes the program to
delete a previously created CHKLIST.MS file which contains
information about each file to include its size, date of creation,
attributes and checksum. In addition, the program will automatically create a new CHKLIST.MS file and will use that file to
alert you to changes made to a file since a previous "Detect" or
"Clean" option selection. The "Virus List" option provides you
with a list of viruses the program has been developed to recognize as well as the ability to search for information about a
specific virus.

Selection of the "Delete" or the "Clean" option in Figure 3.9
results in the display of a window similar to that shown in Figure 3.10. As the scanning process proceeds, the program displays a growing horizontal bar which indicates the percentage
of the scanning process that has been completed. As the bar
grows, the program continuously updates the file being
scanned, the directory in which the file resides, as well as the
summary totals indicated in the lower left portion of Figure
3.10. Upon completion of the scanning process the program displays summary statistics similar to those illustrated in Figure
3.11.

Note that in addition to indicating statistical information concerning disks and disk files scanned, the statistics screen indicates the time required for the scan. Once you use the program
a few times you will obtain an appreciation for the time required

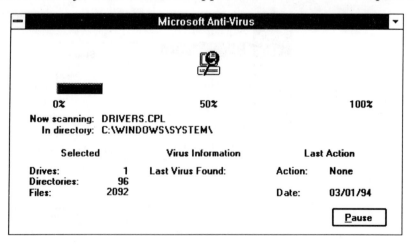

Figure 3.10   The Microsoft Anti-Virus scanning process.

Statistics				
	Scanned	Infected	Cleaned	OK
Hard Disks	1	0	0	
Floppy Disks	0	0	0	
Total Disks	1	0	0	
COM Files	116	0	0	
EXE Files	434	0	0	
Other Files	1923	0	0	
Total Files	2473	0	0	
Scan Time	00:05:21			

Figure 3.11 The Anti-Virus program displays summary statistics after each Detect or Clean operation.

for disk scanning based upon the number of files residing on your disk.

One of the more interesting features of the Microsoft Anti-Virus program is its Virus List. As previously noted, you can select the "Virus List" option from the Scan menu. Doing so results in display of the Virus List window similar to that illustrated in Figure 3.12. In that window the "Search for:" box func-

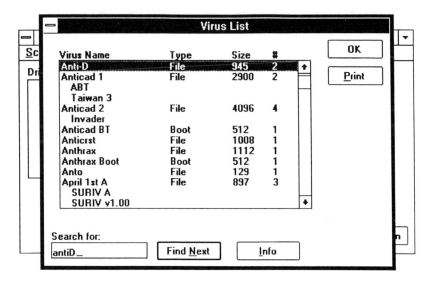

Figure 3.12 The Microsoft Anti-Virus Virus List window.

tions as a searching mechanism to locate a virus in the virus list and not as a mechanism to search your disk for a specific virus. On double-clicking an entry in the window, entering a virus name in the "Search for:" box, or clicking on the "Info" button, the program will display information about a selected virus. Figure 3.13 illustrates the "Information About Virus" window after the Anti-D virus was selected in Figure 3.12. Note that in addition to providing you with the ability to detect and clean viruses, Microsoft's Anti-Virus program can be used as a tutorial to obtain information about a large number of viruses—how they operate, their length and their side effects.

Since the scanning of files for tell-tale code that is characteristic of attack software requires prior knowledge of identifying portions of code, scanning software developers are basically limited to developing programs that can detect known destructive software. This means that an ingenious hacker who develops a new type of destructive program will more than likely have the program escape detection when scanning software is used. This also means that if the destructive software takes a new approach, its operation after activation may bypass the ability of detection programs to initially identify a software attack until some destruction of data occurs. Hence your level of protection against viruses and other types of attack software decreases in time if your anti-viral program is not regularly updated. It is also

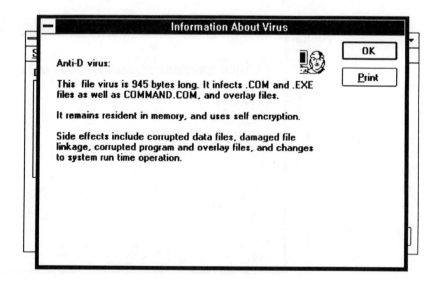

Figure 3.13 Displaying information about the Anti-D virus.

important to recognize the symptoms of attack software and the steps you can perform to minimize the effect of an attack.

Infection symptoms

A number of symptoms serve as a warning that your computer is under attack. Some are quite obvious, such as the display of a message that may contain profanity, attack a politician or display a similar unexpected and unwarranted message. Other symptoms, such as the activation of a disk drive for no apparent reason and the illumination of the drive's light emitting diode, may be much more difficult to note as an indication that your computer is under attack.

Table 3.3 lists nine of the more common indicators that your computer has an unexpected visitor. If one or more of these symptoms should occur there are several actions you should perform and other actions you may wish you had performed unless you were fortunate enough to prepare yourself to recover from different types of disasters.

Recovery operations

One of the most important things to understand when you observe an indication that unwanted software is operating on your computer is that, whatever harm that can happen has already occurred and your actions from this point onward can prevent further harm from occurring. Unless the unwanted program has taken control of your computer and is writing continuously to disk, do not power off your computer. If you

Table 3.3 Common infection indicators.

Programs take longer to load or execute than before.
Disk accesses appear to be excessive for normal tasks.
Disk drives are activated for no apparent reason.
Programs that worked before do not work.
Programs or data files appear to disappear mysteriously.
The use of a utility program shows the presence of mysterious hidden files.
You notice an unexpected reduction in available disk space.
You notice the appearance of an inappropriate message on your screen or
    strange sounds come from your speaker.
Less memory appears to be available for program execution than normal.

---

were not using a virus scanner and have a program available for use, run it. The chances are high that if you have a virus or another type of attack program its techniques may be recognized and the scanner can locate the program. If a scanner is not available or fails to locate any abnormal software, reboot your system using an original system diskette which loads a good write-protected copy of DOS, since the original system diskette is permanently write-protected.

Using the newly loaded operating system, attempt to examine the files you used during the operation which resulted in an infection indicator. For example, did you previously execute a DOS command stored as an .EXE file and a directory listing shows both .COM and .EXE files? If so, the obvious cause of the problem is now apparent. However, what happens if you cannot access your hard drive owing to the modification of your boot sector, FAT, or directory structure?

Although it is probably preferable to have used a disk recovery program which keeps an image of your key hard drive sectors on another area of your drive to facilitate data recovery, you can also attempt to use the DOS command SYS C:, which will rewrite your DOS boot sector on your hard drive if that area was modified.

If this still does not fix the problem and persons you consult shrug their shoulders when asked what you should do next, you may be faced with having to reformat your drive and reload your software that was previously backed up on a regular basis. Although this represents a situation most of us will rarely have to encounter, if you have to reload previously backed up software it is important to recognize that the cause of your problem may also have been placed on your backup tape during your last backup operation. However, since you were able to notice an infection symptom you also noted an operation you performed which caused the symptom. Thus, after you reload your software, reboot from a write-protected copy of DOS and attempt to locate and eliminate the cause of your problem.

3.6 LAN PROTECTION

Since this book is focused upon local area networks, this chapter concludes by discussing software developed to provide protection to the most important part of your network, which is your file server.

Several software developers have introduced products that not only scan the server but, in addition, are designed to keep viruses off the network. The features of network compliant anti-virus products typically include a scanning mechanism that can be set to scan every incoming and outgoing file, preschedule scans, perform manual scans at any time or scan specific types of files, such as all executable files.

Since it is important to notify an appropriate user or group when unwanted software is detected, network compliant products normally enable the network administrator to set the program to either broadcast a message or interface with an electronic mail system to deliver a message to a specific network user.

The most common types of network anti-virus products operate on both the server and client workstations. For example, on a NetWare server the anti-virus product would operate as a NetWare Loadable Module (NLM), while on the client workstation the software might be loaded from a statement in an AUTOEXEC.BAT file and function as a filter which examines computer operations and precludes modifications to key disk areas, such as the boot sector. Some of the client and server programs communicate with each other, providing network administrators with reports concerning workstation users that for one reason or another may not be using anti-virus protection, were identified using a modem, or provide other information which may enable a network administrator to isolate the probable cause of a network infection attempt.

EQUIPMENT AVAILABILITY CONSIDERATIONS

When working with a local area network, the ability to access data quickly can be critical to the success of different organizational activities. Commodity traders, foreign exchange specialists, and persons in similar occupations must have immediate access to programs and data—they usually cannot tolerate an inability to access information for even short periods, since such a situation could occur when a trader was bidding on the sale of thousands of tons of aluminum, exchanging millions of Pesos for Francs, or performing another capital-intensive operation. In other organizations the inability to access LAN facilities may disrupt productivity, result in lost sales or simply become a matter of user inconvenience.

Regardless of the effect of LAN outages, most readers will want to consider one or more methods to reduce the probability of their occurrence. In doing so you will want to examine the effect of different equipment configurations upon the ability of network users to access data if one or more devices should fail. Thus, what you need to facilitate that process is a mechanism to denote the effect of different equipment configurations upon the ability to access network resources. That mechanism is known as "availability" and is the general topic to be covered in this chapter.

We will first define the term and its related terms. Once this is accomplished we will apply the concept to local area networks by first considering the LAN as a grouping of components or devices arranged in sequences of serial or parallel structures. This will illustrate the mathematics involved in computing availability without having to examine different LAN configurations. It will also provide the tools and knowledge to determine the level of availability for different network structures. This knowledge will be applied to compute the availability of different key LAN structures, such as redundant file servers, redundant disk arrays, or redundant communications equipment and transmission facilities used to interconnect geographically separated networks.

A key use of availability is to answer the general question "Is extra hardware or communications facilities warranted?" To answer that, it is necessary first to determine the extra level of availability obtained from the use of additional hardware or communications facilities, and compare that increase in availability to the associated cost. The examples contained in this chapter will serve as a guide to performing the required analysis.

4.1 AVAILABILITY

Just as "one person's passion is another person's poison", there are different ways in which we can look at and define availability. To avoid any possibility of confusion, let us first define the term as it relates to both components and systems. Once this is accomplished, we can examine its applicability to data stored on different local area network structures accessed from different network locations.

Component availability

The availability of an individual component can be expressed in two ways which are directly related to one another. First, as a percentage, availability ($A\%$) can be defined as the operational time of a device divided by the total time, with the result multiplied by 100. This is indicated by the following equation:

$$A\% = \frac{\text{operational time}}{\text{total time}} * 100$$

For example, consider a network file server which normally operates continuously 24 hours per day. Over a one-year period let us assume the server failed once and required eight hours to repair. During the year the server was available for use 365 days times 24 hours/day less 8 hours, or 8752 hours. Thus, the server was operational for 8752 hours during a period of 8760 hours. Using our availability formula we obtain:

$$A\% = \frac{8752}{8760} * 100 = 99.91\%$$

MTBF and MTTR

Let us now define two commonly used terms and discuss their relationship to operational time and total time. The first term, Mean Time Before Failure (MTBF), is the average operational time of a device prior to its failure.

When a device fails, actions are initiated to effect its repair. The time from when the device fails until it is repaired is known as the "time to repair" and the average of each repair time is known as the Mean Time To Repair (MTTR). Since the total time is MTBF + MTTR, we can rewrite our availability formula as follows:

$$A\% = \frac{MTBF}{MTBF+MTTR} * 100$$

It is important to remember the M in MTBF and MTTR, as you must use the average or mean time before failure and average or mean time to repair. Otherwise, your calculations are subject to error. For example, if your file server failure occurred halfway through the year, you might be tempted to assign 4380 hours to the MTBF. Then, you would compute availability as:

$$A\% = \frac{4380}{4380+8} * 100 = 99.91$$

The problem with the above computation is the fact that only one failure occurred, which results in the MTBF not actually representing a mean. Although the computed MTBF is correct for one particular file server, as sure as the sun rises in the East, the MTBF would be different for a second server, different for a third server, and so on. Thus, if you are attempting to obtain an availability level for a number of devices installed or to be installed, in effect you will compute an *average* level of availability through the use of an average MTBF.

The next logical question is how to obtain average MTBF information for file servers, disk arrays, modems, communications circuits, and other network components whose operations affect your ability to access network facilities?. Fortunately, many vendors provide MTBF information that you can use instead of waiting for a significant period of time to obtain appropriate information.

Concerning the MTTR, this number is also provided by the manufacturer but normally requires a degree of modification to be realistic. Most manufacturers quote a figure based upon the time required to repair a device once a technician is onsite. Thus, you must consider the travel time from a vendor's location to your location. If your organization has a maintenance contract which guarantees a service call within a predefined period after notification of an equipment failure, you can use that time period and add it to the MTTR.

For example, assume the specification sheet for a vendor's disk array listed a MTBF of 50 000 hours and a MTTR of 2 hours. If you anticipate installing the disk array in Macon, GA, and the nearest vendor service office is located in the northern suburbs of Atlanta, you would probably add four to six hours to the MTTR time. This addition would reflect the time required for a repair person in Atlanta to receive notification that he or she should service a failed device in Macon, complete his or her work in Atlanta, and travel to the site in Macon. While this may not be significant when a MTBF exceeds a year, suppose your equipment location was Boise, ID, and the disk array vendor required three days to arrange for a service representative to arrive at your Idaho office. In this situation you may have to add 72 hours or more to the time required to repair a typical disk array failure in Boise, to obtain a more realistic MTTR value.

System availability

A system is a collection of individual components or devices arranged in a given structure. By adding additional components to the system and rearranging their structure you can change its level of availability with respect to access by a network user.

To determine the availability of a system you must consider the availability of each device or component and transmission facility interconnecting devices, as well as the overall topology of the system. Concerning the latter, system availability will depend on whether components are connected in series or in parallel. Several basic local area network structures in which devices are connected in series and in parallel will be examined here.

4.2. DEVICES CONNECTED IN SERIES

The top portion of Figure 4.1 illustrates the connection of n components in series. In this and subsequent illustrations a component will be considered to represent either a physical device or a transmission facility connecting two devices. Thus, the boxes labeled A_1, A_2 and A_3 could represent the availability of a modem (A_1), the availability of a leased line (A_2), and the availability of a second modem (A_3). Similarly, the boxes could

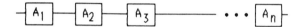

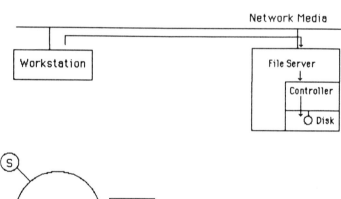

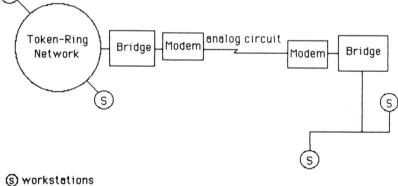

Ⓢ workstations

Figure 4.1 Devices connected in series.

also represent the availability of a file server (A_1), the availability of a disk controller (A_2), and the availability of a disk (A_3) connected to the file server via the insertion of the disk controller in the file server and its cabling to an internal or external disk.

The availability of components connected in series is computed by multiplying the availabilities of the individual components. Mathematically, this is expressed as follows for n components:

$$A = \prod_{i=1}^{n} A_i$$

Disk storage availability

To illustrate the computation of availability for a system in which components are arranged in series, consider the disk installed in a file server which is connected to an Ethernet LAN. This networking system is illustrated in the middle portion of Figure 4.1.

The routing of a workstation user's request to retrieve information stored on the server's disk will flow from the workstation to the file server. From the file server the request will be converted by the disk controller into a series of instructions which position the read/write heads of the disk to retrieve the requested information. Failure of the workstation, network media, file server, controller, or disk would affect the ability of the workstation user to retrieve data. Further, since the workstation and file server are each connected to the local area network through adapter cards, we must also consider the operational status of these. Thus there is a requirement to determine the availability of seven distinct devices to compute the availability of stored data on the file server (see Table 4.1).

Since the connection between the workstation and the file server's disk is represented by seven devices connected in series, the availability of disk data storage to a workstation user becomes:

$$A = A_1 * A_2 * A_3 * A_4 * A_5 * A_6 * A_7$$

One of the major problems associated with determining the accessibility of data stored on a local area network involves

Table 4.1 Availability components for server disk accessibility.

Availability components	Availability level
Workstation	A_1
Workstation LAN adapter	A_2
Network media	A_3
File server	A_4
File server LAN adapter	A_5
File server disk controller	A_6
File server disk	A_7

whether or not you should consider each component. The failure of a LAN adapter card at a workstation can easily be compensated for by a user moving to another workstation. Similarly, many cable failures are momentary in duration, caused by an inadvertent pull on a cable. For many network managers, access to data stored on a file server is normally reduced to an examination of the availability levels of the major components of the server—its LAN adapter card, controller, disk, and the file server itself.

As an example, assume MTBF and MTTR values as indicated in Table 4.2. These are for illustrative purposes only, although they are fairly representative. (As already noted, MTTR values can vary significantly depending upon the type of maintenance contract your organization may have with a hardware service provider, the distance from your office to a vendor's service center, the time a component failure occurs and, if repair is by shipping a replacement device, the ability of your location to obtain next day delivery from Express Mail, Federal Express, or another express delivery service. Based upon the MTBF and

Table 4.2 Representative MTBF and MTTR values for computing disk data accessibility.

Component	MTBF	MTTR
LAN adapter card	43 800	2
Controller	35 040	16
Disk	43 800	36
File server	52 560	24

MTTR values listed in Table 4.2 the availability of data stored on the file server becomes:

$$A\% = \left(\frac{43800}{43802}\right) * \left(\frac{35040}{35056}\right) * \left(\frac{43800}{43836}\right) * \left(\frac{52560}{52584}\right) * 100 = 99.82$$

Internetwork access

Another important area of concern is accessibility to data on another network. When networks are connected by a local bridge, you can obtain the MTBF and MTTR values for the bridge and consider that as an additional component connected in series. However, when networks are geographically separated from one another you must then consider the availability of several networking devices as well as the transmission facility linking the two networks.

To illustrate this, assume a Token-Ring network connected to an Ethernet network via remote bridges and modems as illustrated in the lower portion of Figure 4.1. Assume that each remote bridge has a MTBF of one year, or 8760 hours, and any failure would be corrected by the manufacturer shipping a replacement unit to each location where a bridge is installed. Thus, we might assume a worst-case MTTR of 48 hours to allow for the time between reporting a failure and the arrival and installation of a replacement unit. Similarly, let us assume a MTBF of 8760 hours and a MTTR of 48 hours for each modem. For the transmission line, most communications carriers specify a 99.5% level of availability for digital circuits, so using a slightly lower level of 99.4% for an analog circuit would appear to be reasonable. The availability of the communications system, A_S, which enables a user on a Token-Ring network to access the Ethernet network and vice versa via a pair of single-port bridges, then becomes:

$$A_S\% = [(Bridge_A)^2 * (Modem_A)^2 * Line_A] * 100$$

where:

$Bridge_A$ is the availability level of each bridge
$Modem_A$ is the availability level of each modem
$Line_A$ is the availability level of the analog circuit connecting the two locations.

Since the availability of each component is its MTBF divided by the sum of the MTBF and the MTTR, we obtain:

$$A_S\% = \left(\frac{8760}{8808}\right)^2 * \left(\frac{8760}{8808}\right)^2 * 0.994 * 100 = 97.25\%$$

This means that 2.75% of the time (100 − 97.25) in which an attempt is made to use the communications system, the failure of one or more components will render the system inoperative.

We can use the two earlier computations to obtain the availability of data stored on a file server on one network with respect to a workstation user located on a different network. Since the two separate systems, file storage and WAN interconnection of LANs are represented by components in series, we can multiply the computed availability of each system to obtain the availability of data stored on the file server of one network with respect to a workstation user located on the other network. If $A_{DN}\%$ represents the availability of data on the file server of one network with respect to a workstation user located on the other network, then:

$$A_{DN}\% = (0.9982) * (0.9725) * 100 = 97.07\%$$

4.3. DEVICES CONNECTED IN PARALLEL

The top portion of Figure 4.2 illustrates n devices connected in parallel. If only one device out of n is required to provide access to stored data or a communications path between networks at any point in time, then the availability of the system as a percentage becomes:

$$A_S\% = \left[1 - \prod_{i=1}^{n} (1 - A_i)\right] * 100$$

For example, assume two devices each having an availability level of 99.0% are operated in parallel. Then, the availability level of the resulting parallel system becomes:

$$A_S\% = \left[1 - \prod_{i=1}^{2} (1 - A_i)\right] * 100$$

a. Schematic representation

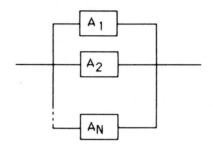

b. File server with dual controllers and disk drives

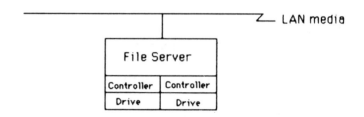

c. Schematic representation of mirrored disk controllers and disk drives

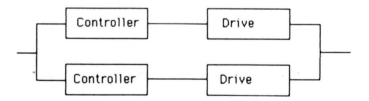

Figure 4.2 Devices connected in parallel.

Substituting, we obtain:

$$A_S\% = [1 - (1 - 0.99) * (1 - 0.99)] * 100 = 99.99\%$$

In a local area network environment, there are several types of common equipment configurations which represent parallel devices. We can cite the use of dual controller cards in file servers to provide access to a pair of mirrored disk drives. (The term "mirrored disk drives" refers to the fact that data recorded on one drive is duplicated on the second drive. Readers are referred to Chapter 5 for specific information concerning different types of data storage protection methods, including the use of mirrored drives.) The middle portion of Figure 4.2 illustrates the connection of a file server containing dual disk controllers and mirrored disk drives to a LAN.

One of the key questions network managers, analysts and designers have concerns the difference in the level of availability between single and dual disk storage systems. To illustrate how you can use the preceding formulas to answer this question, we can use the MTBF and MTTR data previously listed in Table 4.2. Since we currently want to focus our attention upon the use of single or dual disk subsystems, including the disk controller and disk, let us temporarily defer consideration of the availability level of the file server and its network adapter card.

For a single disk subsystem represented by a disk controller and disk in series, the availability of the subsystem is computed as follows:

$$A\% = \left(\frac{35040}{35056}\right) * \left(\frac{43800}{43836}\right) * 100 = 99.87\%$$

For the dual disk subsystem represented by two disk controllers and disk drives operated in parallel, the availability level of the equipment can be represented by two pairs of serially connected devices connected in parallel as illustrated in the lower portion of Figure 4.2. Then, the availability level of each parallel path is exactly the same as the single disk subsystem consisting of one disk controller and one disk drive connected in series. Thus, the availability level of the two parallel disk controllers and disk drives becomes:

$$A\% = [1 - (1 - 0.9987) * (1 - 0.9987)] * 100 = 99.9998\%$$

Thus, the use of dual controllers and disk drives increases the availability level of the disk subsystem from approximately 99.87% to 99.99%, a difference of 12 hundredths of a percent. Whether or not the increase in the level of availability of mirrored controllers and disk drives is worth the additional cost depends upon your organization's requirements to access data and its budget.

Considering the file server as an entity

Let us now focus our attention upon the file server as an entity, to include the server and the network adapter card installed in the server. From a schematic perspective the availability of stored data to a network user would resemble Figure 4.3a if there were only one disk controller and one disk drive in the server, while Figure 4.3b would represent the availability level of components when the server has dual disk controllers and a pair of mirrored disks.

From Table 4.2 we note that the availability of the LAN adapter card is 43800/43802, while the availability of the file server is 52560/52584. When we consider the file server storage system as an entity to include the availability level of the LAN adapter card and the file server, we can compute the availability levels of single and dual disk subsystem based file servers as follows:

Single disk subsystem file server
$A\% = (43800/43802) * (52560/52584) * (0.9987) * 100 = 99.81$

Dual disk subsystem file server
$A\% = (43800/43802) * (52560/52584) * (0.9999) * 100 = 99.94$

a. Single controller and disk drive

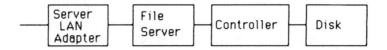

b. Dual controllers and disk drives

Figure 4.3 Considering file server storage availability as an entity.

As one would intuitively expect, when you consider the availability level of the file server as an entity the difference between the use of single and dual disk subsystems in the server narrows. In fact, the less reliable the file server or adapter card the narrower the difference in availability between the use of single and dual disk subsystems. Recognizing this fact, many users with true mission-critical applications will operate mirrored servers, a topic also discussed in Chapter 5.

4.4 DUPLICATING COMMUNICATIONS PATHS

In the lower portion of Figure 4.1, a serial communications path was illustrated connecting a Token-Ring network to an Ethernet network. In performing an analysis to determine an appropriate method to duplicate communications paths between geographically separated LANs, network managers, analysts and designers can consider two methods. One method involves the use of completely duplicated facilities to include hardware and communications facilities. A second method involves the use of pairs of single dual port bridges or routers connected to duplicate communications equipment and transmission facilities.

The rationale for considering the use of a pair of single dual port bridges or routers is based upon cost and availability levels of the components of a communications path. Concerning cost, the duplication of bridges or routers may involve a considerable expenditure of funds. Concerning availability levels of the components in a communications path, leased lines will normally experience an average of four to six outages of varying durations during the year. In comparison, communications equipment is usually an order of magnitude more reliable. Thus, many organizations will prefer to have duplicate communications circuits connected to common bridges or routers.

Figure 4.4 compares two common methods used to provide communications redundancy between geographically dispersed local area networks. Although bridges are shown in Figure 4.4, routers could be used in place of bridges. That is, the two networks could be interconnected through the use of two pairs of single port routers or one pair of dual port routers. If bridges are used, readers should note that transparent bridging supported by Ethernet networks precludes the use of closed loops which physically occur through the use of dual bridges or multi-port bridges illustrated in Figures 4.4a and 4.4b. However, if we

a. Full redundancy

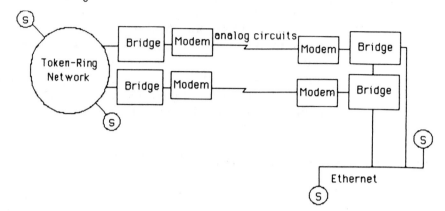

b. Partial redundancy

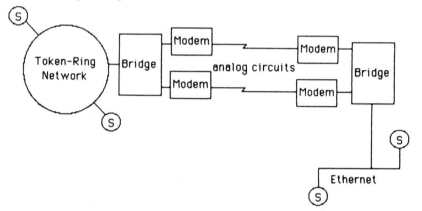

Figure 4.4 Common methods used to obtain communications redundancy between geographically separated LANS.

assume that only one path operates at a single point in time, the use of two paths in which one only becomes active if the other becomes inactive is supported by transparent bridging.

In the topology illustrated in Figure 4.4a, duplicate remote bridges, modems and transmission paths are installed. In Figure 4.4b it is assumed that an organization could obtain a very reliable remote bridge and preferred to expend funds on parallel communications circuits and modems since, as previously discussed, the failure rate of long distance communications facilities normally exceeds the failure rate of equipment.

Full redundancy

For simplicity, let us assume that the availability level of each component illustrated in Figure 4.4a is 90%. For each parallel path we can consider the traversal of the path to encounter five components: two bridges, two modems, and the communications line. Thus, the upper path containing five devices in series would have an availability level of 0.9 * 0.9 * 0.9 * 0.9 * 0.9, or 0.59049. Similarly, the lower path would have a level of availability of 0.59049. Thus, we have now reduced the network structure to two parallel paths, each having an availability level of 59.049%. If A_1 is the availability level of path 1 and A_2 is the availability level of the second path, the communications system availability, A_S, becomes:

$$A_S\% = \left[1 - \prod_{i=1}^{2} (1 - A_i) \right] * 100$$

Thus:

$$A_S\% = [1 - (1 - A_1)(1 - A_2)] * 100$$

Simplifying the above equation by multiplying the terms and substituting 0.59049 for A_1 and A_2, we obtain:

$$A_S\% = (A_1 + A_2 - A_1 * A_2) * 100 = 83.23\%$$

Partial redundancy

Now let us focus our attention upon the network configuration illustrated in Figure 4.4b, in which a common bridge at each LAN location provides access to duplicate transmission facilities. To compute the availability of this communications system, we can treat each bridge as a serial element, while the two modems and the communications line between each modem represent parallel routes of three serial devices.

Figure 4.5 shows how we can consider the communications system previously illustrated in Figure 4.4b as a sequence of serial and parallel elements. By combining groups of serial and parallel elements we can easily compute the overall level of availability for the communications system, as indicated in

a. Original topology with indicated availability levels of network
   components and transmission facilities

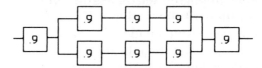

b. Combining availability of serial components in parallel

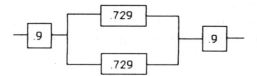

c. Combining availability of parallel components

d. Resulting availability level of communications system

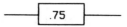

Figure 4.5 Computing the availability level of a mixed topology communications system.

parts a, b, c and d of Figure 4.5. In Figure 4.5b the three serial elements of each parallel circuit were combined, including the two modems and communications line, to obtain a serial availability level of 0.9 * 0.9 * 0.9, or 0.729. Next, in Figure 4.5c the two parallel paths were combined to obtain a joint availability of 0.729 + 0.729 – 0.729 * 0.729, or 0.926. Finally, the joint availability of the parallel transmission paths was treated as a serial element with the two bridges, obtaining a system availability of 0.75, or 75%.

Note that at a uniform 90% level of availability for each device the use of single bridges versus dual bridges lowers the system availability by approximately 8%. That is, the communications system availability obtained through the use of dual single-port bridges illustrated in Figure 4.4a was computed to be 83.23%, while the system availability obtained from the use of single dual-port bridges illustrated in Figure 4.4b was determined to be 75%.

Dual hardware *versus* dual transmission facilities

Previously the availability of two similar but slightly different local area network bridging configurations which differed in their use of dual bridges versus the use of a multiport bridge were computed. Assuming a uniform component availability of .90 the system availability of the dual network illustrated in Figure 4.4a was computed to be 83.23%, while the availability of the network illustrated in Figure 4.4b was computed to be 75%. Although the difference in availability of over 8% obtained in the example could probably justify the extra cost associated with dual bridges for organizations with critical applications, what happens to the difference in the availability of each network as the availability level of each component increases?

Table 4.3 compares the system availability for the use of single multiport and parallel single-port bridge networks as component availability increases from 0.90 to 0.999. Note that the difference between the availability level of each network

Table 4.3 System availability comparison.

Component availability	System availability	
	Single multiport bridge	Parallel single-port bridges
0.90	0.7505	0.8323
0.91	0.7778	0.8586
0.92	0.8049	0.8838
0.93	0.8318	0.9073
0.94	0.8582	0.9292
0.95	0.8841	0.9488
0.96	0.9094	0.9659
0.97	0.9337	0.9800
0.98	0.9571	0.9908
0.99	0.9792	0.9976
0.999	0.9980	0.9999

configuration decreases as component availability increases. In fact, the 8% difference in the availability at a component availability level of 0.90 decreases to under 4% at a component availability level of 0.98 and to under 2% at a component availability level of 0.99. Since most modern communications devices have a level exceeding 0.99 (which, by the way, usually exceeds the availability level of a transmission facility by 0.005), the use of dual bridges instead of multiport bridges may be limited to increasing network availability by one-tenth of 1%. Thus, you must balance the gain in availability against the cost of redundant bridges.

Concerning cost, although bridges vary considerably with respect to features and price, at the beginning of 1995 their average price was approximately $3000. In comparison, the incremental cost of a dual-port bridge versus a single-port bridge was typically less than $500. Since you require two bridges to link geographically separated networks, the cost difference between the use of dual single-port bridges and single dual-port bridges is approximately (3000 – 500) * 2, or $5000. Thus, in this example you would have to decide if an increase in network availability by approximately 0.1% is worth $5000.

If your organization operates a reservation system in which a minute of downtime could result in the loss of thousands of dollars of revenue, the additional cost would probably be most acceptable. If your organization uses your network for inter-office electronic mail transmission, you might prefer to save the $5000 and use single dual-port bridges instead of dual single-port bridges. This is because a gain of 0.1% of availability based upon an eight-hour workday with 22 workdays per month would only provide 2.1 additional hours of availability per year. At a cost of approximately $3500 per hour for the additional availability, it might be more economical to simply delay non-urgent mail and use the telephone for urgent communications.

4.5 INTERNETWORK DATA ACCESS AVAILABILITY

We can determine the availability of data stored on one network with respect to a workstation user located on another network by considering communications system availability and file server availability. We would first compute the availability level of data storage on the file server to be accessed. Next, we would compute the communications system availability. Since the relationship between the communications system and the data stored on the file server can be considered as systems in series, we would then multiply the previously computed availability levels together. This will provide the availability of data stored on one network with respect to a workstation user located on another network.

For example, consider the file server previously illustrated in Figure 4.3b which contains dual controllers and disk drives and whose availability level was computed to be 99.94%. Assume that the file server is located on the Token-Ring network illustrated in Figure 4.4a, while a user who requires access to that data is located on the Ethernet network illustrated in that diagram. Since the availability level of the communications system linking the two networks was computed to be 83.23%, the availability of data stored on the file server on the Token-Ring network with respect to a workstation user on the Ethernet network becomes:

$$A\% = (0.9994) * (0.8323) * 100 = 83.13\%$$

Readers are reminded that the communications path availability between the Token-Ring and Ethernet networks illustrated in Figure 4.4a was computed based upon a uniform component availability of 90%. That level of availability was selected arbitrarily for illustrative purposes and you would want to use component availability levels that more accurately reflect the specifications of equipment and transmission facilities you anticipate using to connect networks.

4.6 AUTOMATING AVAILABILITY COMPUTATIONS

The computation of whole system availability can be reduced to a string of computations for devices in series and parallel. To facilitate these computations involved in determining serial and parallel component availability, the program AVAIL.BAS was developed (Figure 4.6)

The program can be used to compute the availability levels for components connected in series or in parallel. In fact, by selecting the program's BOTH option, it will first compute the availability level of components connected in series and then compute the availability level of components connected in parallel.

```
CLS : REM PROGRAM AVAIL.BAS
PRINT "PROGRAM AVAIL.BAS TO COMPUTE AVAILABILITY LEVELS"
PRINT
PRINT "INDICATE COMPUTATIONS DESIRED "
PRINT "  S)ERIAL"
PRINT "  P)ARALLEL"
PRINT "  B)OTH SERIAL AND PARALLEL"
RGN:   INPUT "ENTER THE TYPE OF COMPUTATIONS DESIRED      : ", COMP$
:F COMP$ <> "S" AND COMP$ <> "P" AND COMP$ <> "B" THEN GOTO AGN:
:F COMP$ = "B" THEN TRY$ = "A"
:F COMP$ = "B" THEN COMP$ = "S"
GOSUB DENTER
:F COMP$ = "S" THEN GOSUB SCOMPUTE
:F COMP$ = "P' THEN GOSUB PCOMPUTE
:F TRY$ = "A" THEN COMP$ = "P"
:F TRY$ = "A" THEN GOSUB DENTER
:F TRY$ = "A" THEN GOSUB PCOMPUTE
GTOP
DENTER:
              IF COMP$ = "P" THEN GOTO PAR
              INPUT "ENTER NUMBER OF COMPONENTS IN SERIAL -MAX 10  : ", C
              IF COMP$ = "S" THEN GOTO SER
PAR:          INPUT "ENTER NUMBER OF COMPONENTS IN PARALLEL -MAX 10 : ", C
SER:          PRINT : PRINT "HOW DO YOU WANT TO ENTER DATA ?"
              PRINT "AS P)ERCENT E.G. 12.5"
              PRINT "AS M)TBF AND MTTR"
              INPUT "ENTER DATA ENTRY METHOD -P OR M            : ", D$
              IF D$ <> "P" AND D$ <> "M" THEN GOTO DENTER
              IF D$ = "M" GOTO MENTRY
              FOR I = 1 TO C
              PRINT "FOR COMPONENT"; I;
              INPUT "ENTER PERCENT AVAILABILITY     : ", A(I)
              A(I) = A(I) / 100
              NEXT I
              RETURN
MENTRY:
              FOR I = 1 TO C
              PRINT "FOR COMPONENT"; I;
              INPUT "ENTER MTBF AND MTTR VALUES   : ", MTBF(I), MTTR(I)
              A(I) = MTBF(I) / (MTBF(I) + MTTR(I))
              NEXT I
              RETURN
SCOMPUTE:
              IF COMP$ = "P" GOTO PCOMPUTE
              PROD = 1
              FOR I = 1 TO C
              PROD = PROD * A(I)
              NEXT I
              PRINT USING "AVAILABILITY OF ## "; C;
              PRINT USING " DEVICES IN SERIES = ##.#####"; PROD * 100
              RETURN
```

Figure 4.6   AVAIL.BAS program listing (in BASIC).

```
PCOMPUTE:
          PROD = 1
          FOR I = 1 TO C
          PROD(I) = (1 - A(I))
          PROD = PROD * PROD(I)
          NEXT I
          AVAIL = 1 - PROD
          PRINT USING "AVAILABILITY OF ##"; C;
          PRINT USING " DEVICES IN PARALLEL = ##.#####"; AVAIL * 100
          RETURN
END
```

Figure 4.6 Continued.

To facilitate data entry, the program permits you to enter data in either of two ways. You can enter data concerning the availability level of individual components as a percentage or you can enter MTBF and MTTR values. For either data entry method the program accepts a maximum of 10 component availability values, which should be more than sufficient for essentially all network configurations.

If you require the computation of more than 10 component availability values, you can easily modify AVAIL.BAS. To do so you would simply add a DIM statement at the beginning of the program which would contain a value for each array used in the program that reflects the highest number of components you intend to analyze. Since BASIC automatically dimensions all arrays to 10 elements, no DIM statement was required in AVAIL.BAS.

Program execution

Since the best way to illustrate the use of a computer program is to execute it, let us do so. Let us assume our network configuration consists of two sets of five components connected in series, with each set routed parallel to the other set of components. Let us also assume that we have component availability expressed as a percentage for one set of components and as MTBF and MTTR data for the second set.

Figure 4.7 illustrates the execution of AVAIL.BAS to compute the availability of five serially connected components when availability for each component is available as a percent. In this example, it was assumed that four components each had an

```
PROGRAM AVAIL.BAS TO COMPUTE AVAILABILITY LEVELS

INDICATE COMPUTATIONS DESIRED
   S)ERIAL
   P)ARALLEL
   B)OTH SERIAL AND PARALLEL
ENTER THE TYPE OF COMPUTATIONS DESIRED                    : S
ENTER NUMBER OF COMPONENTS IN SERIAL -MAX 10              : 5

HOW DO YOU WANT TO ENTER DATA ?
AS P)ERCENT E.G. 12.5
AS M)TBF AND MTTR
ENTER DATA ENTRY METHOD -P OR M                          : P
FOR COMPONENT 1 ENTER PERCENT AVAILABILITY               : 99.9
FOR COMPONENT 2 ENTER PERCENT AVAILABILITY               : 99.9
FOR COMPONENT 3 ENTER PERCENT AVAILABILITY               : 99.85
FOR COMPONENT 4 ENTER PERCENT AVAILABILITY               : 99.9
FOR COMPONENT 5 ENTER PERCENT AVAILABILITY               : 99.9
AVAILABILITY OF 5 DEVICES IN SERIES = 99.45120
```

Figure 4.7 Execution of AVAIL.BAS to compute the availability of serially connected devices using the percentage availability method of data entry.

availability level of 99.9%, while one component had an availability level of 99.85%. As noted at the bottom of Figure 4.7, the availability level of the five devices in series was computed to be 99.45%.

Figure 4.8 illustrates the execution of the program AVAIL.BAS to compute the availability of five serially connected components when you wish to use and have available MTBF and MTTR data. In this example it was assumed that four network components each had a MTBF of 8000 hours and a MTTR of 24 hours. Concerning the latter, it was assumed that repair was accomplished by replacement and that the organization used an overnight service to deliver a new device to replace a failed device. Since the presumed experience is that the average time from failure notification to the replacement of the failed device is 24 hours, 24 was used for each of four MTTR values. The fifth component had a MTBF of 720 hours and a MTBR of 2 hours. This availability setting is representative of many digital transmission lines, since there are 24 * 30, or 720 hours in a month, and one 2-hour failure provides an approximate 99.7% level of line availability. As indicated at the bottom of Figure 4.8, the availability level of this second set of five devices connected in series was computed to be 97.95%.

```
PROGRAM AVAIL.BAS TO COMPUTE AVAILABILITY LEVELS

INDICATE COMPUTATIONS DESIRED
  S)ERIES
  P)ARALLEL
  B)OTH SERIAL AND PARALLEL
ENTER THE TYPE OF COMPUTATIONS DESIRED              : S
ENTER NUMBER OF COMPONENTS IN SERIAL -MAX 10        : 5

HOW DO YOU WANT TO ENTER DATA ?
AS P)ERCENT E.G. 12.5
AS M)TBF AND MTTR
ENTER DATA ENTRY METHOD -P OR M                     : M
FOR COMPONENT 1 ENTER MTBF AND MTTR VALUES          : 8000,24
FOR COMPONENT 2 ENTER MTBF AND MTTR VALUES          : 8000,24
FOR COMPONENT 3 ENTER MTBF AND MTTR VALUES          : 720,2
FOR COMPONENT 4 ENTER MTBF AND MTTR VALUES          : 8000,48
FOR COMPONENT 5 ENTER MTBF AND MTTR VALUES          : 8000,48
AVAILABILITY OF 5 DEVICES IN SERIES = 97.95843
```

Figure 4.8 Execution of AVAIL.BAS to compute the availability of serially connected devices using the MTBF and MTTR method of data entry.

Now that we have determined the availability level of each set of serially connected devices, we can compute the whole system availability by treating it as two devices in parallel. Thus, we can use AVAIL.BAS one more time, and compute the system availability level of your two sets of five serially connected devices. To do so you will execute AVAIL.BAS and select the parallel computation option.

Figure 4.9 illustrates this with the parallel option selected. Since the previous executions of AVAIL.BAS resulted in two availability levels expressed as a percentage, we now select the percentage data entry method for the parallel component computations. As indicated in Figure 4.9, the result is an overall availability level of 99.98874%. This represents the system availability level of the two sets of five serially connected components whose individual availability levels were previously specified. As indicated by this short example.

You can thus use the program AVAIL.BAS to simplify the computations associated with different network structures since those structures can be considered to represent a mixture of devices connected in series or parallel.

```
PROGRAM AVAIL.BAS TO COMPUTE AVAILABILITY LEVELS

INDICATE COMPUTATIONS DESIRED
  S)ERIAL
  P)ARALLEL
  B)OTH SERIAL AND PARALLEL
ENTER THE TYPE OF COMPUTATIONS DESIRED            : P
ENTER NUMBER OF COMPONENTS IN PARALLEL -MAX 10    : 2

HOW DO YOU WANT TO ENTER DATA ?
AS P)ERCENT E.G. 12.5
AS M)TBF AND MTTR
ENTER DATA ENTRY METHOD - P OR M                  : P
FOR COMPONENT 1 ENTER PERCENT AVAILABILITY        : 99.4512
FOR COMPONENT 2 ENTER PERCENT AVAILABILITY        :
                                                  97.94843

AVAILABILITY OF 2 DEVICES IN PARALLEL = 99.988
```

Figure 4.9 Execution of AVAIL.BAS to compute the availability of parallel connected devices.

5

DATA STORAGE
PROTECTION

In this chapter we turn our attention to methods and techniques we can use to protect stored data. We will first examine the use of Hot Fix areas, disk mirroring, disk duplexing, and different types of redundant arrays of inexpensive disks, more commonly referred to as RAID levels. We then look at methods we can use to backup LAN data and the role of the uninterruptable power supply (UPS) in minimizing the effect of power outages and voltage spikes upon stored data.

5.1 GENERAL DATA STORAGE PROTECTION METHODS

There are a number of general data storage protection methods that are incorporated into network operating systems to provide different levels of integrity to file server data. In this section we examine the general operation of Hot Fix redirection, mirroring and disk duplexing, and in the next section we look at their initialization under Novell Corporation's NetWare operating system.

Hot Fix areas

A Hot Fix area is a portion of disk space used for data storage redirection when one or more data storage areas on a disk become defective. Under NetWare and other network operating systems, a Hot Fix Redirection Area or similarly named disk space is created automatically when an operating system partition is created on a server. The resulting Hot Fix Redirection

Area then becomes available to hold data blocks that are redirected to that location as the operating system encounters bad blocks of storage located in the main data storage area of the disk.

A logical question to ask is "How does a network operating system determine that a particular block in the main data storage area of the disk is faulty?" The answer to that question is the use of read-after-write verification, similar to the familiar /V option many readers use with the DOS COPY command.

Read-after-write verification results in the network operating system on the server immediately reading back from disk the contents of each block it writes to disk. When the operating system reads the data, it compares its content to the original data block stored in memory. If the data read from disk matches the contents of the data in memory the write operation is considered to have been performed without error and data stored in memory is released. This frees that memory location for use by subsequent file server operations. If data read from disk does not match the data in memory, the network operating system will perform a predefined number of retries, rereading the contents of the data block and comparing the data reread to the data in memory. After the number of predefined retries is reached and data retrieved from the disk still does not match the data in memory, the network operating system considers the disk storage block to be defective. At this time the network operating system's Hot Fix feature will redirect the original data block which is still stored in memory to the Hot Fix Redirection Area, where the data can be stored without error. Then, the network operating system records the address of the defective block in a portion of the Hot Fix area reserved for that purpose, which in future operations permits it to bypass attempting to store data in a defective disk area. Figure 5.1 summarizes the steps involved in the use of a Hot Fix Redirection Area.

Safeguarding other data storage locations

Although a Hot Fix area can be considered as a mechanism to safeguard data as it is recorded, it does not protect data against damage due to future electromechanical disk operations. For example, a power surge or spike, a sudden loss of power, or another abnormality, such as vibration from the movement of furniture, could adversely affect the movement of the read/write

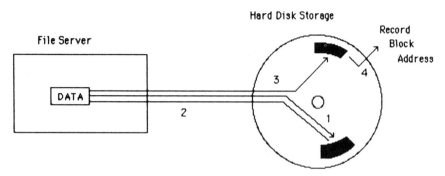

1. Block of data written from memory to disk
2. Read-after-write verification operation
3. If read-after-write verification fails data is written to
   the Hot Fix Redirection Area block
4. Bad block location recorded

Figure 5.1 Using a Hot Fix Redirection Area.

heads of a disk. If the resulting effect was to damage or destroy a hard disk's file allocation table (FAT) or directory, it might be very difficult or impossible to obtain access to previously stored information.

Recognizing the criticality of directory and FAT address information, many network operating systems maintain duplicate copies of both the directory table and FAT on separate areas of a file server's hard drive.

If a data storage block containing directory or FAT information is subsequently damaged, the operating system will switch to retrieving information from the duplicate set of tables. The operating system then marks the faulty locations and stores copies of the duplicate set of tables in another location on the disk to maintain a usable backup set of tables. NetWare automatically provides a duplication of directory tables and FATs which is user-transparent and imbedded into the operating system. Two additional data protection features built into NetWare include disk duplexing and disk mirroring.

Disk duplexing

Disk duplexing represents the process of copying data onto two hard disks through separate disk channels. In a NetWare operating system environment in which file servers are PC-type computers, this means that separate controller cards or separate disks with built-in controllers are used to obtain a disk duplexing environment. Figure 5.2 illustrates the hardware components associated with disk duplexing as well as the flow of data from the file server to its disk storage.

Disk duplexing also provides the hardware configuration which enables a network operating system to enhance its data retrieval operation. For example, Novell NetWare uses a disk duplexing environment to perform split seeks, a technique in which read requests are sent to one disk in a pair that is not busy at the time of the request. This permits faster data retrieval, since separate disk channels permit the file server to perform multiple, simultaneously overlapping read operations.

The major advantage of disk duplexing is that it permits continuity of operations when any component, from a disk channel to a device on a disk subsystem, becomes inoperative. Under NetWare, the operating system uses the alternative disk channel path while transmitting a warning message to indicate the occurrence of a disk failure.

Of course, disk duplexing does not ensure data protection, since the simultaneous failure of both hard disks could result in the loss of data. Thus, disk duplexing serves as a mechanism for increasing data storage availability but should not be considered as a substitute for the orderly backup of server data.

Disk mirroring

Disk mirroring can be considered as a more elementary method of protecting data, falling in between the use of a Hot Fix Redirection Area and disk duplexing.

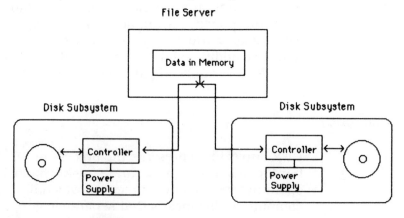

Figure 5.2 Disk duplexing.

Under disk mirroring, two or more hard disks on the same channel are paired, with one disk being designated as the primary device, the other a secondary device. Blocks of data written to the primary disk are also written to the duplicate disk, a technique referred to as mirroring data.

Figure 5.3 illustrates the hardware configuration. Note that unlike disk duplexing which uses separate channels to access separate disk subsystems, disk mirroring involves the use of a common channel to the stored data. This technique does not protect you from a channel failure, which would result in an inability to access data on both disks. In addition, without the use of separate channels, read operations can only be overlapped based upon buffer storage, if any, in the controller. Since the results of all read operations return to the file server via a single channel, the ability to access information is not as fast as when disk duplexing is used.

As with disk duplexing, mirroring provides protection for data storage and accessibility in the event one drive should fail. However, like disk duplexing, disk mirroring by itself does not ensure data protection and is no substitute for the backup of data on a regular basis.

5.2 WORKING WITH NETWARE

Although NetWare includes several built-in data protection features, with the exception of Hot Fix they must be initialized for use. In addition, the default allocation of file space under Net-

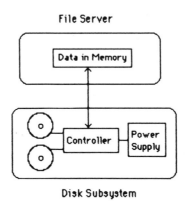

Figure 5.3 Disk mirroring.

Ware is 98% for data and 2% for the Hot Fix Redirection Area. Thus, if you want to consider using another built-in data protection feature or to modify the Hot Fix Redirection Area storage allocation, you must use the NetWare INSTALL program.

Using INSTALL

INSTALL is a menu driven program which provides the ability to format and mirror hard drives, create NetWare partitions, change the file space allocated to data storage and the Hot Fix Redirection Area, and perform other related operations. Since the primary focus of this chapter is upon data storage protection techniques and methods, we will examine the use of INSTALL for those features.

Figure 5.4 illustrates the program's main menu. This program is provided by Novell and a NetWare Loadable Module (NLM). Thus, it must be loaded from the console of the server or by a person who has remote console rights so that he or she can load it at their workstation.

Selecting the "Disk Options" entry in the "Installation

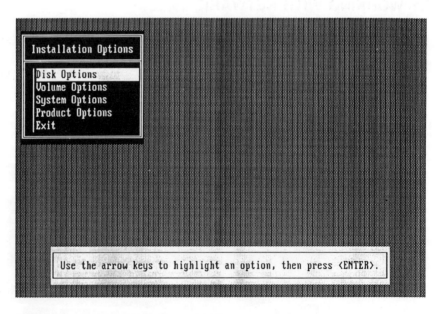

Figure 5.4 NetWare INSTALL program's main menu.

Options" window results in the display of a new selection menu slightly superimposed on the prior window. Figure 5.5 illustrates this window which is appropriately labeled "Available Disk Options", as it provides you with the ability to select from three related disk processes. The first time you use this program during the installation of NetWare you would define the types of disk drives and create any required partitions. Thus, selecting the "Partition Tables" option will result in the display of previously defined disk drives.

Figure 5.6 illustrates the resulting "Available Disk Drives" window, which is superimposed upon the previously displayed window. By moving the highlight bar over an appropriate entry and pressing the Enter key, you cause the INSTALL program to select a previously defined disk drive. This results in the display of two new windows which are illustrated in Figure 5.7. The upper window, which is not labeled, displays information concerning the partitions on the selected disk. The lower window, which is labeled "Partition Options", provides you with the ability to create and delete partitions, return to the previous menu, or change the Hot Fix storage allocation. Since we are interested in examining NetWare utilities that provide us with

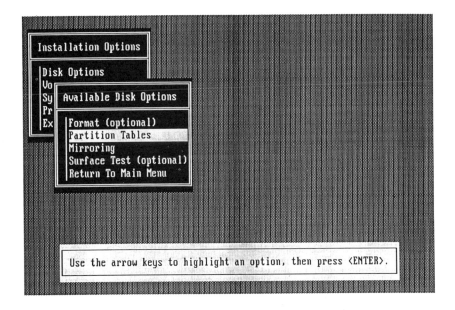

Figure 5.5 INSTALL program's Available Disk Options menu.

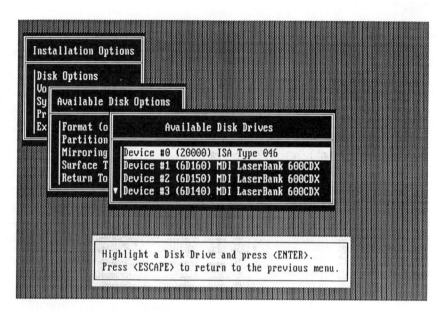

Figure 5.6 Using the INSTALL program to select a disk drive.

the capability to protect data, let's select the "Change Hot Fix"
entry in the "Partition Options" menu.

Changing the Hot Fix allocation

Selecting the "Change Hot Fix" option shown in Figure 5.7
results in the display of a window labeled "Partition Information" which is illustrated in Figure 5.8. That window displays
information concerning the NetWare partition for the selected
disk, and provides the ability to alter the relationship between
the allocation of storage for data and the allocation of storage
for the Hot Fix Redirection Area.

When you select the "Create NetWare Partition" from the "Partition Options" window in Figure 5.7, NetWare creates a partition and allocates a default of 98% of the space to data storage
and 2% to the Hot Fix Redirection Area. To change the allocation
relationship, you should select the "Change Hot Fix" option to
display the "Partition Information" window shown in Figure 5.8.
To change the size of either area you should move the highlight
bar over the field you wish to change. Then, you enter the num-

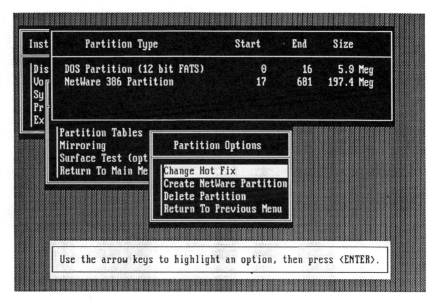

Figure 5.7 Using INSTALL to change the Hot Fix storage allocation.

ber of new blocks for either field and the program computes remaining space in the other field and adjusts the number of Mbytes for the data area and percentage displayed for the redirection area. Now that we are familiar with how to use INSTALL to adjust hot fix information let's turn our attention to the use of this program for mirroring or duplexing the partitions on two or more hard disks.

Mirroring or duplexing partitions

To mirror or duplex the partitions on two or more hard disks, you would select the "Mirroring" option from the "Available Disk Options" window illustrated in Figure 5.5. Doing so results in the display of a window labeled "Partition Mirroring Status", which indicates whether or not logical partitions are mirrored. From that window you would select the primary logical partition to be mirrored or duplexed, which would result in the display of a window labeled "Mirrored NetWare Partitions" superimposed upon the previous window.

Figure 5.9 illustrates the sequence of display of four windows from "Installation Options" to "Mirrored NetWare Partitions".

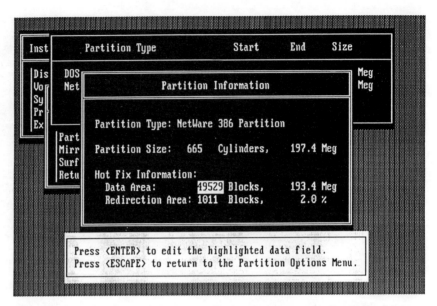

Figure 5.8 The Partition Information window indicates the allocation of storage between the data and redirection areas as well as providing the ability to change the allocation.

Pressing the Insert key when the "Mirrored NetWare Partitions" screen is displayed provides you with the ability to add a partition to a mirrored set. The result of pressing the Insert key is the display of a window labeled "Available Partitions", from which you would select the secondary partition to be mirrored or duplexed.

NetWare SFT

Novell NetWare provides an additional level of data storage protection which is extended to the complete file server. Referred to as System Fault Tolerance (SFT), this version of NetWare represents an operating system which provides complete redundancy by mirroring both the file server and its data storage. Not only does SFT prevent downtime due to a server hardware failure but, in addition, provides you with the ability to perform a server maintenance upgrade without bringing down the network.

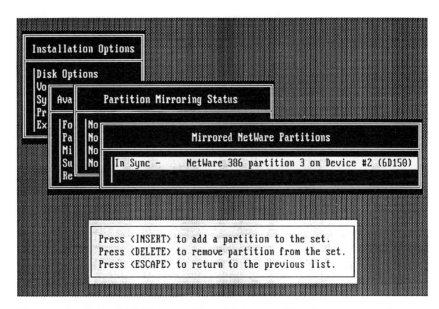

Figure 5.9 Using INSTALL to add or delete a partition from a mirrored set.

Novell's current fault tolerance product, SFT III, requires the use of two identical 80386 or higher performance servers with a minimum of 12MB of RAM per server. Each server is connected to the network by separate LAN adapter cards, although each server uses the same IPX address, resulting in the two servers having a single appearance on the network.

Under SFT III, servers are connected to one another through the use of Mirrored Server Link (MSL) adapter cards. Each MSL card provides access for server synchronization and must be an EISA or Micro Channel adapter which supports a 32-bit data transfer and has connectors for coax or fiber cable, permitting synchronization between servers at data rates up to 100Mbps. One server is configured to operate as a primary server, while the second operates as a secondary server. Figure 5.10 illustrates SFT III server mirroring on a Token-Ring network.

Since each server has an identical network address, data transmitted from each workstation flows to both servers. As long as the primary server is operational, the secondary server ignores all network file requests. If the primary server should fail, the secondary server detects the failure and then becomes the primary server.

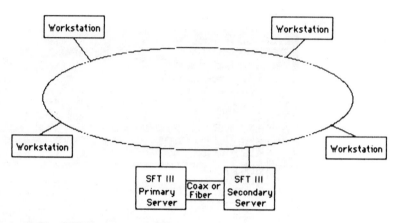

Figure 5.10   SFT III server mirroring.

Server mirroring alternatives

Although SFT III extends mirroring from disk storage to a complete file server its cost can be considerable. In addition to the duplication of file server hardware, you must obtain special MSL adapters as well as Novell's SFT III software.

One viable alternative to the use of SFT III   for organizations that have mission-critical operations and want to consider mirrored servers is the use of third party mirroring utility software. Mirroring utility software operates on each client workstation, using the local NetWare shell to direct file server requests to two servers, with each server having a different LAN address. Figure 5.11 illustrates the use of a mirroring utility to obtain a server mirroring capability.

The use of mirroring software on each workstation eliminates the necessity for specialized hardware or upgrading existing servers. However, the use of mirroring utility software doubles network activity, which can adversely effect network performance. In addition, the use of mirroring software requires two licenses for the servers the utility software redirects requests to, and the utility on each client reduces memory available to run applications.

5.3. COMPARING DATA STORAGE AVAILABILITY

Through the application of availability formulas presented in Chapter 4, we can compare and contrast disk duplexing and mirroring.

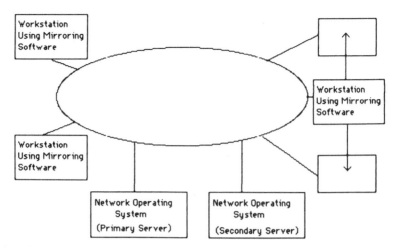

Figure 5.11   Using mirroring utility software to mirror servers.

Let us assume that the mean time before failure of a hard disk is 30 000 hours and a controller has a MTBF of 50 000 hours. Assume that the mean time to repair (MTTR) for a disk represents the time to replace a disk plus the time required to restore data by loading it onto the disk, while the MTTR for a controller represents the time to replace the controller. If we assume both a disk and controller can be obtained via an overnight express delivery service, a reasonable MTTR for the disk could be 36 hours, while a reasonable MTTR for the controller could be 30 hours.

For the disk drive, its availability becomes:

$$A\% = \frac{MTBF}{MTBF + MTTR} * 100 = \frac{30000}{30000 + 36} * 100 = 99.88\%$$

For the disk controller, its availability becomes:

$$A\% = \frac{MTBF}{MTBF + MTTR} * 100 = \frac{50000}{50000 + 30} * 100 = 99.94\%$$

From an availability perspective, a disk controller and disk represent two components in series. When disk mirroring is employed the controller is used to read to and write from two disks that can be represented as parallel components. Hence, disk mirroring can be graphically represented by a controller in series with two parallel disks as illustrated in the top portion of

Figure 5.12. Since two separate controllers are used with disk duplexing, this method of data storage protection can be represented by two parallel paths of serially placed components as illustrated in the lower portion of Figure 5.12.

Disk mirroring The availability of the two disks in parallel is computed as follows:

$$A\% = [1-(1-0.9988)(1-0.9988)] * 100 = 99.99986\%$$

Since the parallel disks are in series with the single controller, the availability of the mirroring system is computed as follows:

$$A_S\% = 0.9994 * 0.9999986 * 100 = 99.9399\%$$

Disk duplexing Now let's focus our attention on disk duplexing. As illustrated in the lower portion of Figure 5.12 the availability level of disk duplexing is represented by two pairs of serial components in parallel. The availability of a controller and disk in series is computed as follows:

a. Disk mirroring

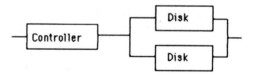

b. Disk duplexing

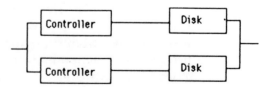

Figure 5.12 Graphical representation of disk mirroring *versus* disk duplexing availability.

$$A\% = (0.9994 * 0.9988) * 100 = 99.82\%$$

Then, the availability of the two pairs of parallel components which represent the system availability level is computed as follows:

$$A_S\% = [1-(1-0.9982)(1-0.9982)] * 100 = 99.9997\%$$

In comparing the availability level of disk mirroring to disk duplexing our intuition that dual controllers and drives used by duplexing provides a higher level of availability is verified.

However, for the MTBF and MTTR values used for the computations, note that disk duplexing's availability level exceeds that obtainable from disk mirroring by just 0.06% (99.9997 − 99.9399. While this additional level of availability is more than justified against the additional cost of hardware for mission-critical applications, it may be hard to justify for LANs primarily used for document sharing, electronic mail and network printer utilization—applications in which a telephone can provide backup for short periods of server unavailability.

MTBF considerations

Concerning the MTBF values for disk drives, the calculations to compare availability of disk mirroring versus disk duplexing assumed a MTBF value of 30 000 hours, which represents approximately four years of operational service.

When examining a vendor's MTBF statistics on a disk drive specification sheet, readers may be surprised to find figures ranging from 100 000 hours to 250 000 hours, or more. The chances are very high that those figures represent *extrapolated* disk performance based upon the testing and analysis of individual components as they are exposed to a range of hostile environments, including shock and vibration, high and low temperatures and power on and off cycles.

While high MTBFs are impressive, the tests performed by a vendor to provide a foundation for life cycle analysis of disk components may not be fully representative of conditions that can occur in a typical office. For example, a power surge or an inadvertent mating of the mail cart with the desk holding a file server could result in an inoperative disk much earlier than an extrapolated estimate.

One key question to ask yourself when considering a vendor's MTBF claim is why their warranty is a fraction of its MTBF. After all, a MTBF of 250 000 hours represents a period of approximately 28.5 years. Yet, most vendors limit their warranty period to 3 or 5 years! Based upon this, when analyzing the availability levels of disk mirroring versus disk duplexing you may want to consider using the warranty period in place of a vendor's extrapolated MTBF.

5.4 RAIDS

Redundant arrays of inexpensive disks (RAIDs) represent a technology that was developed as an economical method for obtaining fault-resilient disk storage. The original definition of RAID, which occurred at the University of California, Berkeley, in 1987, defined a five-level architecture, with each level representing a different measure of performance, storage capacity and resilience. Since its original definition, vendors have added extensions to RAID technology to provide enhanced levels of fault-tolerant disk storage capabilities.

Although the storage capacity of a physically small disk was typically limited to 100M bytes or less in 1987, by 1994 disks used in RAID technology were capable of providing storage of 1GB or more. This expansion resulted in the technology becoming a critical component for moving key business applications from mainframes onto local area networks.

RAID levels

Although the paper published at Berkeley in 1987 defined the term RAID and described an architecture that defines five RAID levels, that paper did not explicitly address what constitutes an array. In general, any disk subsystem architecture which combines two or more standard, physical disk drives into a single logical drive to obtain a level of fault-tolerant data redundancy can be considered to represent a disk array. Thus, an array can represent two, three, four, or more disk drives. What is important under RAID is the method by which data is recorded onto each drive that forms an array.

RAID Level 0

RAID Level 0 was not included in the University of California paper as it does not provide redundancy. Under RAID Level 0, data is written across all drives used to form the disk array in a predefined order, as illustrated in Figure 5.13. This method of data recording in which data is written across multiple disks instead of one is referred to as "data striping".

In examining RAID Level 0 data storage allocation illustrated in Figure 5.13 note that while there is no data redundancy capability, Level 0 enhances performance by providing for balancing random I/O requests among all drives in a disk array. Thus, RAID Level 0 is primarily used in applications where data integrity is not critical but disk performance is. Since the failure of any disk in the array results in the inability of data to be retrieved, the MTBF for the array is reduced to the MTBF of a single drive divided by the number of drives in the array. For example, if the MTBF of each drive in a four-drive disk array is 40 000 hours, then the MTBF of the array is 40 000/4, or 10 000 hours.

Data is stored in blocks across all of the disks that make up the array. Although RAID Level 0 facilitates quick read and write times for large data files, it offers no protection in the event a disk becomes inoperative.

From a physical perspective, RAID Level 0 can be considered to represent the connection of n disks cabled to a common disk controller installed in a host computer. Figure 5.14 illustrates the physical cabling of drives in a RAID Level 0 disk array. Note

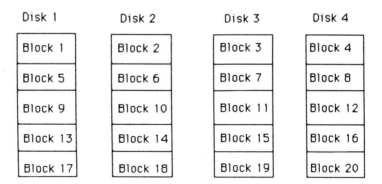

Figure 5.13   RAID Level 0 data allocation.

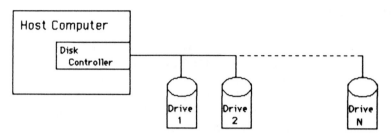

Figure 5.14 Physical cabling of drives in a RAID Level 0 disk array.

that since each drive is normally contained in a separate enclosure, each drive in a RAID Level 0 disk array normally has its own power supply.

RAID Level 1

RAID Level 1 is commonly referred to as "mirrored" or "shadowed" disks. This is because data stored on one disk is duplicated onto a second disk through the use of a common controller. Thus, if either drive in a pair should fail, the disk array can continue to provide access to data from the remaining drive in the pair.

Figure 5.15 illustrates an example of RAID Level 1 data allocation for a four-disk array. As indicated, a block for block duplication of stored data on the first drive in each pair is created on the mirrored drive.

Although RAID Level 1 permits read requests to be spread over both disks in a paired set, the mirroring offers no improvement in performance when writing data. In addition, since one

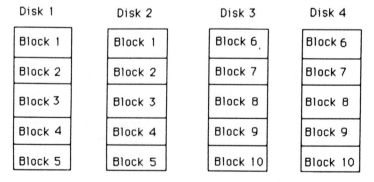

Figure 5.15 RAID Level 1 data allocation.

disk completely backs up another, the overhead of this pairing reduces the usable storage capacity of two drives to 50% of their total storage, or as expected, one drive's storage capacity.

From a physical perspective, RAID Level 1 resembles RAID Level 0 since both levels involve the use of a common disk controller to control multiple disks in a disk array. Although many RAID Level 1 disk arrays use only two disks, other common Level 1 disk arrays consist of four, six or eight disks, representing two, three and four pairs of mirrored disk drives.

RAID Level 2

RAID Level 2 represents the first RAID level which provides for data integrity through the use of error-correcting parity codes. Under RAID Level 2, data is written across all of the disks in an array, similar to the manner in which data is stored under RAID Level 0. However, data storage differs in two important areas.

First, data is written across all data storage disks in the array one byte or bit at a time, whereas RAID Level 0 records data in blocks across all pairs of disks in the disk array. Secondly, an error-correcting parity code is generated and stored, which enables the reconstruction of lost data if one of the drives in the disk array should fail. The key to this data reconstruction is obtained from the use of the exclusive OR (XOR) function to generate parity.

Data reconstruction Figure 5.16a illustrates the values obtained from an XOR operation upon two variables. As indicated, XOR produces a true (1) result if either but not both variables are true, while XOR produces a false (0) result if both variables have the same value or setting. Since the XOR operation can be applied against data stored on separate drives, it provides a mechanism to reconstruct data in the event any one in N drives fail.

To illustrate how data can be reconstructed, let us assume there are three drives in our disk array labeled A, B and C. Further assume that the first bit recorded in block n of each drive was 1, 0 and 1, respectively. Then, A XOR B results in a value of 1. If we then XOR the intermediate result against the value of the data stored on drive C, 1 XOR C, we obtain 0, which becomes the parity across the array for bit position 1 in block

a. XOR Operation

A	B	A XOR B
0	0	0
0	1	1
1	0	1
1	1	0

b. Applying XOR Operations
Generating Parity

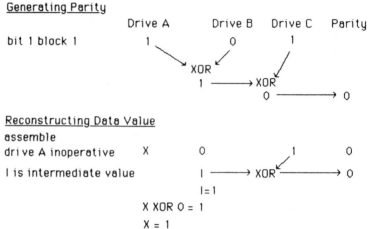

Figure 5.16 RAID data reconstruction.

n. The first line of data in Figure 5.16b indicates the results of the previously described XOR operations which generate a parity value of 0.

Next, assume drive A failed. Since A XOR B yields an intermediary result (I) which is XORed with C's value of 1 to yield a parity value of 0, we can work backwards to determine the value of A. That is, for I XOR C to have a value of 0, I must have a value of 1. Then, for A XOR B to have a value of 1 when B has a value of 0 requires A to have a value of 1.

Thus, we are able to reconstruct the value of bit position 1 in block *n* if drive A fails, and would then continue the same procedure to reconstruct other data previously stored on the failed drive. It is left for the reader to verify that similar procedures will result in the reconstruction of data from drives B or C if either should fail but not both simultaneously.

Under RAID Level 2, three extra disks in the array are used exclusively to store parity codes, using a technique similar to but more complex than just described. This provides a mechanism for data to be reconstructed in the event data corruption

Disk 1	Disk 2	Disk 3	Disk 4	Disk 5	Disk 6	Disk 7
Bit/Byte 1	Bit/Byte 2	Bit/Byte 3	Bit/Byte 4	Parity	Parity	Parity
Bit/Byte 5	Bit/Byte 6	Bit/Byte 7	Bit/Byte 8	Parity	Parity	Parity
Bit/Byte 9	Bit/Byte 10	Bit/Byte 11	Bit/Byte 12	Parity	Parity	Parity
Bit/Byte 13	Bit/Byte 14	Bit/Byte 15	Bit/Byte 16	Parity	Parity	Parity
Bit/Byte 17	Bit/Byte 18	Bit/Byte 19	Bit/Byte 20	Parity	Parity	Parity

Figure 5.17 RAID Level 2 data allocation.

should occur. Figure 5.17 illustrates the allocation of data under RAID level 2.

RAID Level 3

RAID Level 3 duplicates the method of data storage provided by RAID Level 2 with one exception. Instead of using three extra disks to store parity, Level 3 uses one parity drive. This reduction in the number of parity drives is accomplished by adding intelligence to each disk in the array so that they can detect corrupted data, which reduces the quantity of information required to be stored on the parity drive. The reduction in the number of drives makes a RAID Level 3 array more economical than a Level 2 array. One of the more common RAID Level 3 configurations is a disk array containing five drives. Four drives are used for data storage while the fifth stores parity.

RAID Level 4

RAID Level 4 can be considered to represent RAID Level 0 with a parity drive. That is, under RAID Level 4 data is written in blocks across all of the disks used for data storage in the disk array, with an extra drive used for parity storage.

Although the use of error-correcting parity in RAID Levels 2, 3 and 4 adds a degree of data integrity, the storage architecture is ill-suited for certain applications. For example, the retrieval of small size data blocks requires a relatively large overhead for the retrieval of data stored in small pieces across multiple disks.

Thus, typical client server applications, including database field updates, directory retrievals, and other transaction-oriented applications, are rarely used with RAID Levels 2, 3 and 4, significantly limiting the market for those types of RAIDs.

RAID Level 5

Under RAID Level 5, data is striped across multiple drives on a block basis similar to RAID Level 0. However, parity correcting code information is stored on a different disk from the data to which the parity correcting codes refer.

Figure 5.18 illustrates an example of RAID Level 5 data allocation. Note that Level 5 eliminates the necessity for having a separate drive for parity code storage. The distribution of parity information across all drives enables a RAID Level 5 system to operate with one non-operational disk so that recovery does not have to be performed immediately. However, prior to data recovery the Level 5 system with one failed disk is no longer fault-tolerant. Thus, recovery of data for a failed drive must occur prior to a second drive failure to prevent the loss of data. Also note that disk array I/O performance is enhanced in comparison with the use of a single drive, since multiple read and write operations can be performed simultaneously.

In the event of a disk failure, the missing data from the failed disk can be re-created from the data and parity correcting codes stored on the remaining operational drives in the disk array. Thus, RAID Level 5 provides protection against data loss due to a single drive failure without requiring one or more drives for

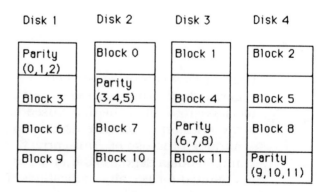

Figure 5.18   RAID Level 5 data allocation.

parity storage or mirroring of data. The overhead resulting from the storage of parity information can vary from approximately 12% to 33% of the total formatted capacity of the disk array, with the actual amount of overhead based upon the number of disks in the array.

RAID Level 6

RAID Level 6 is similar to RAID Level 0 in that it represents an extension to the originally defined RAID levels. Although RAID Level 6 was not standardized when this book was written, several vendors had introduced products based upon an evolving specification.

A basic definition of RAID Level 6 is RAID Level 5 plus redundant controllers and mirroring on a block basis across drives. This results in RAID Level 6 representing a combination of Level 5 in which parity is spread across multiple drives, Level 1 in which drives are mirrored, and Level 0 in which data is striped across drives in blocks.

One of the key features of RAID Level 6 is its ability to support mirroring on an odd number of disks. This becomes possible since mirroring is performed at the block level, which results in data always being mirrored on at least two drives. However, no two drives are identical. This means that if two drives fail RAID Level 6 may be able to continue operating, but its ability to do so depends upon which two drives should fail. If the failed drives do not represent fully mirrored data, operations can continue, otherwise RAID Level 6 will be similar to other levels in its inability to protect against multiple drive failures.

RAID Level 10

Level 10 represents another extension to the original University of California series of disk array design specifications. It obtains its name from the fact that it represents a hybrid implementation of Level 0 and Level 1. Thus, RAID Level 10 represents a combination of data block striping and data mirroring. Data striping is normally performed at the operating system level, while mirroring is performed by the disk controller controlling a pair of disks.

From a performance perspective, Level 10 provides a disk I/O capability similar to Level 0. From a data redundancy and fault-tolerance perspective, Level 10 is similar to Level 1. From a cost perspective, Level 10 is more expensive than Level 0 and may be slightly more expensive than Level 1. This is because a four-disk array under RAID Level 0 would result in the use of eight disks in a Level 1 disk array. Although eight disks would also be required in a Level 10 disk array, any additional cost for data striping for the Level 10 disk array would result in a higher cost than a Level 1 disk array.

Disk array evaluation

The evaluation of disk array systems can be a complex task which may considerably exceed the evaluation of stand-alone disks. This is because you first have to decide upon an appropriate RAID level to satisfy your requirements prior to evaluating competitive disk array products.

Once that is accomplished the evaluation of competitive systems will still be more complex than for stand-alone disks. This is because you must consider both individual disk specifications as well as their aggregate under the disk array structure developed by each vendor and certain physical attributes, such as cabinet size, applicable to disk array housings.

Table 5.1 provides a comprehensive list of disk array specifications readers can use as a guide in evaluating this category of data storage equipment. Included in this table is a column in which you can enter your specific requirements as well as two columns in which you can compare disk array specifications from two vendors against your requirements.

Table 5.2 summarizes the methods you can consider to directly protect data stored on a disk. As previously noted in this chapter, you can employ multiple techniques. However, the ability to do so will depend upon your network operating system's data protection features, the type and capability of disks you use, and any special software required to perform byte or bit striping and the generation of parity correcting codes as a mechanism for data reconstruction.

Note that the last method listed in Table 5.2, server mirroring, can be combined with any or all of the previously listed protection methods. However, as previously noted in this chapter, the mirroring of a server can be expensive both in terms of hardware cost and network performance.

Table 5.1 Disk array specification comparison.

Specification	Your requirement	Vendor A	Vendor B
RAID Level	————	———	———
Cabinet	————	———	———
Dimensions	————	———	———
Number of drives	————	———	———
Formatted drive MB storage	————	———	———
Total array MB storage	————	———	———
Dual power supplies	————	———	———
Removable power supplies	————	———	———
Removable drives	————	———	———
Key lock(s)	————	———	———
Controller bus support	————	———	———
Maximum transfer rate Mbps	————	———	———
OS driver support	————	———	———
MTBF per drive	————	———	———
MTBF for system unrecoverable failure	————	———	———
Replacement warranty	————	———	———
AC power	————	———	———
VA rating	————	———	———
Input watts	————	———	———
Heat dissipation	————	———	———

Table 5.2 Disk storage data protection methods.

Hot Fix Redirection Area
Duplicate directory addresses
Duplicate FAT addresses
Disk duplexing
Disk mirroring
Disk block or bit striping
Use of parity correcting codes
Server mirroring

5.5 TAPE BACKUP

When the first PC systems with hard disks were introduced the backup of data was limited to diskettes. Although it was important to backup critical information, many organizations failed to do so because of the time required to use diskettes.

While archiving software and the use of data compression has increased the efficiency of diskettes as a backup mechanism, increases in hard disk data storage capacity and use has essentially resulted in the use of diskettes as a backup mechanism for a very small fraction of computer installations. Fortunately, tape storage device technology has kept up with advances in hard disk storage and now provides a mechanism to perform backup of critical data.

Storage options

Tape storage devices range in scope from a single portable drive that can be connected to the parallel port of different computers throughout the office, to built-in drives mounted in the system unit of a computer, and tape arrays.

Here the tape array represents a group of tape drives in which data blocks are recorded across all drives in the array for data protection. This technique, which is the same as data striping across disks, permits simultaneous I/O operations to all of the drives in the array and can provide data transfer rates as high as 20–50MB per minute, or more. For large servers the use of a tape array represents a mechanism to minimize the time required for backup and recovery operations.

Drive features

Table 5.3 lists seven tape drive features you may wish to consider prior to acquiring this device for backup and recovery operations. Of course, in the event of a natural or man-made

Table 5.3 Tape drive features to consider.

Interface to computer
Data storage capacity per tape
Recording format
Data transfer rate
Multidrive operations
   Cascading
   Mirroring
   Striping
Data compression
Driver availability

disaster the prior use of a tape drive provides you with a mechanism to restore critical data at another location. However, to do so you need a procedure to store your tape backups at an offsite location on a regular basis, which is a topic discussed later in this chapter.

Although several of the features listed in Table 5.3 are self-explanatory others may require a degree of elaboration. The recording format can be proprietary to a specific vendor or can follow a current or proposed ANSI digital data storage standard. At the time this book was prepared there were several ANSI tape recording standards as well as a tape technology that was in the process of obtaining approval as a standard. The tape technology in the process of being approved by ANSI was Digital Equipment Corporation's digital linear tape (DLT). DLT competes primarily with 8mm and 4mm digital audiotape and provides advantages with respect to storage capacity and transfer rate over the other technologies, as indicated in Table 5.4. DLT was previously approved by the European Computer Manufacturers Association (ECMA) and the International Standards Organization, and the technology is rapidly being incorporated into LAN environments.

Concerning multidrive operations, cascading refers to the automatic writing of data onto a second drive's tape when the prior drive's tape is filled. Tape mirroring is the simultaneous recording of the same data onto two or more tapes, while tape striping, as previously mentioned, represents writing data onto two or more tapes by placing alternate blocks on each tape.

If you use a tape mirroring system you can generate two copies of your backup data at one time, facilitating the transfer of one copy to an offsite storage location. However, if time is of the essence in preparing your backups you may prefer to use a tape striping system and duplicate the tapes after the backup operation is completed.

Perhaps the key drive feature to consider is the availability of

Table 5.4   Tape storage technologies.

Feature	Tape recording technology		
	4mm DAT	8mm	DLT
Non-compressed capacity	4GB	5GB	10GB
Maximum transfer rate	500 Kbps	500 Kbps	1.2 Kbps
Form factor	3.5 inch	5.25 inch	5.25 inch

a driver which is compatible with the network operating system you are using. To illustrate the importance of this feature, let us examine the NetWare NBACKUP utility program.

NetWare's NBACKUP utility program

Included in NetWare is a utility program named NBACKUP that can be used to backup and restore data on file servers and local workstation drives. This program supports the use of a range of media storage devices, including workstation diskette drives, tape and optical drives that have a DOS device driver, workstation hard drives and network drives. You can also back up data to certain non-DOS devices if those devices have available drivers.

When you first execute NBACKUP the program will display a list of available drivers and devices supported. Selecting a device from the list results in its linkage with the NBACKUP utility program and enables its use as a backup mechanism. As you might expect, the use of NBACKUP to backup the file server requires you to have supervisory rights.

After you have selected the storage media for your backup, NBACKUP will display a window labeled "Backup Options", which provides you with the ability to tailor your backup operation. Figure 5.19 illustrates the NetWare backup utility "Backup Options" window whose display occurs after you first select the "Backup Options" entry in the program's Main Menu, followed by selecting the "Backup File Server" option in the window labeled "Backup Menu" which is almost completely obstructed from view by the window labeled "Backup Options".

Table 5.5 elaborates on the backup options displayed in the NBACKUP "Backup Options" window.

Once the backup operation begins, the utility program will present a status window in which information concerning the backup operation is displayed. That window will indicate the data being backed up, the amount of data previously backed up, and the elapsed time of the backup session. When removable media is used for backup, the cartridge number of the tape in use will also be displayed. This provides you with a mechanism to document your backups as well as verify the transfer of appropriate tapes to an offsite storage facility.

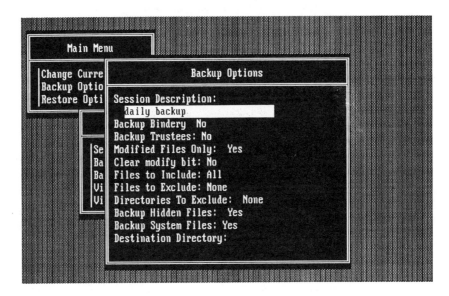

Figure 5.19 NetWare NBACKUP utility program backup options window.

NetWare Storage Management Services

In an attempt to standardize network-based backup, Novell developed software which permits access to data regardless of where it is located or how it is formatted. Known as Storage Management Services (SMS), this product supports Novell's universal tape format specification referred to as System Independent Data Format (SIDF). Theoretically, network users should be able to use SMS to create a backup tape using one vendor's backup system and use that tape in another vendor's product during a restore operation. However, the lack of support of the SIDF format by many vendors, as well as the inability of many products to use "foreign" tapes that do not have a correct header, currently precludes a high degree of tape exchangeability.

SMS is not a backup program. Instead, it was developed as a set of Applications Programming Interface (API) services. Thus, backup programs are developed to use SMS. Novell implemented SMS as a series of server-based NetWare Loadable Modules (NLMs) and client modules. This enables backup pro-

Table 5.5   NBACKUP backup options.

Option	Description
Session Description	Permits you to identify the backup
Backup Bindery	Enables you to backup or bypass the bindery
Backup Trustees	Permits you to backup or bypass the backup of trustee assignments granted to directories and files
Modified Files Only	Permits you to backup only files modified since the last backup.
Clear Modify Bit	Enables you to specify if the "Modified since last archived bit" is cleared
Files to Include	Enables either all or defined files to be backed up
Files to Exclude	Enables either defined files or no files to be excluded from the backup operation
Directories to Exclude	Enables selected directories or no directories to be excluded from the backup
Backup Hidden Files	Enables all or no hidden files to be backed up
Backup System Files	Enables all or no system files to be excluded from the backup operation
Destination Directory	Permits you to specify the location of a DOS device for the backup. If a specific device was previously selected, this option is not displayed

grams, with appropriate security, to backup both client work-stations and servers.

Backup strategy

Although having backup hardware and software is important, of equal importance is a backup strategy. Thus, we will conclude this section by discussing the elements you may wish to consider when formulating a backup strategy.

The success or failure associated with the use of tape backup depends upon the method you use to create the backups, where you locate them, and how you test them.

Backup creation

The frequency with which you perform tape backups depends upon the criticality of your organization's data, its speed of change, and the quantity of data to be backed up. Conventional wisdom says that your LAN should be backed up at least on a daily basis. However, if your daily backup cycle is initiated at midnight, a server failure or another type of disaster that occurs at 5 p.m. could result in the loss of a full day of work. If your LAN is used to store critical information which frequently changes, you might want to consider running a midday backup or implementing a televaulting operation in which files that change are transmitted to an offsite location in real-time or on a near real-time basis. (Readers are referred to Chapter 9 for information concerning televaulting.) Regardless of the method used to duplicate server resident data, you should examine the cost required to duplicate lost work against the cost of more frequent backups.

Some organizations perform frequent incremental backups, where only files changed since the last backup are archived. The incremental backups are used to supplement full saves which occur on a daily or weekly basis. This technique of full and incremental backups can be very effective when servers store gigabytes of data and multiple daily backups may strain the ability of the network to serve its customers. However, incremental backups require a considerable amount of additional management as you now have to keep track of such information as the location and modification of backed-up files. For example, with a daily full save you would only have to locate one copy of each file which resides on the last daily backup. If you perform a weekly full save and daily incremental saves, you could have up to six copies of a file if the file changed each day.

Fortunately, several tape backup vendors are borrowing mainframe data center techniques by marketing tape librarian systems which assist LAN managers and administrators in keeping track of the contents of full saves and incremental saves.

Backup tape location

Some tape library systems include both on-site and off-site tape management capability, including automating media rotation schedules. Regardless of whether or not you use a tape library system, it is important to store copies of your organization's backup tapes at an offsite location. Doing so considerably reduces the risk of a building or server disaster.

When using an offsite storage location you should consider both the tape rotation policy to use as well as whether to maintain duplicate backup tapes on site. One common tape rotation scheme is to exchange tapes on a weekly basis. Concerning duplicate backup tapes, maintaining a second set of tapes on site may provide a more time-responsive ability to recover from inadvertent file erasures, the effects of untested programs, and other human error embarrassments.

Backup testing

Every once in a while you can expect to hear the story of the network administrator who faithfully backed up LAN data and rotated tapes to an offsite storage location. Unfortunately, when disaster struck and tapes were recalled from the offsite storage location, to the network administrator's chagrin the tapes could not be read. The lesson in this story is that it is extremely important to test your backup tapes periodically. In fact, testing should be an integral part of your tape backup plan.

5.6 THE ROLE OF UPS

Disk drives, like other home appliances, are dependent upon electricity to operate. However, unlike such appliances as toasters, ovens and popcorn poppers, the electronics built to control the operation of disk drives as well as other computer components are very sensitive to power fluctuations. This means that, in addition to providing a backup power mechanism to provide servers and other critical network components with the ability to either continue operating or generate an orderly shutdown in the event of a power failure, you will more than likely want to ensure that your equipment is not subjected to surges, spikes, brownouts, and other power abnormalities. Fortunately, modern uninterruptable power supplies (UPS) provide you with the ability to obtain battery backup power as well as regulating AC supplies to protect equipment against utility power abnormalities.

In this section we will first discuss the backup power and power protection features you should examine when considering the use of one or more UPS systems. This will be followed by an examination of a new class of "network aware" UPS systems that provide users with the ability to control certain UPS parameters from a network station as well as for the UPS to broadcast messages to network users.

Backup power

The primary purpose of a UPS system is to provide backup power in the event of a power failure. In a network environment, the use of a UPS system to protect file servers provides you with the ability to avoid situations in which a power failure could result in a read/write head crash. Since most modern hard disks include a head parking mechanism which results in the movement of the read/write heads to a fixed location in the event of a power failure, this mechanism protects data previously stored on the disk from a head crash. However, the mechanism does not protect data in the process of being written to disk. Thus, battery backup power from a UPS system can save data from being lost by providing time for the server to have an orderly shutdown.

Capacity

UPS systems are normally specified in VA (volt-amperes) or kVA and ampere hours (Ah). VA or kVA represent the load the UPS can deliver to operate one or more devices, while Ah specifies the duration for which the UPS can supply the load.

Table 5.6 lists the load in VA for a variety of representative

Table 5.6 VA load for representative communications equipment.

IBM PS/2 model 55SX w/VGA	200
Wellfleet FN router	200
Compaq 386/33 w/VGA	300
IBM PS/2 model 80 server w/VGA	350
Cisco CGS router	350
IBM PS/2 model 95 server w/XGA	375
Compaq SystemPro server	500
IBM AS/400 minicomputer	800
3 COM Linkbuilder 500	900
Wellfleet CN router	1600
Wellfleet BCN router	2000

communications devices, ranging from an IBM PS/2 model 55SX used as a bridge, to different file servers and routers. By first examining the load of equipment you wish to backup and then determining the minimum time you want to keep equipment powered in the event of a primary power failure, you can determine the capacity of the UPS required to satisfy your requirements.

You should consider all equipment, including printers, monitors and external hard drives in addition to the system unit of each computer.

Most devices list their voltage and amperage requirement on a metal plate or in a manual. You can multiply those figures together to obtain the VA requirement of each device. Other equipment may list their power requirements in watts (W). To convert watts to VA you should multiply the watts rating by 1.4. By summing the VA's, you obtain the minimum UPS VA load you require.

Although many network decision makers are tempted to minimize UPS capacity for apparently valid reasons, you may wish to consider other factors that can change an initial equipment selection decision criterion. For example, suppose your organization's LAN includes 50 stations, one file server and a remote bridge which connects the LAN to a distant location. If your building does not already have a UPS system, you might decide that a power failure should be compensated for by protecting the file server for only a few minutes for an orderly shutdown, since other network users within the building could not access the server. However, if your server has information critical to network users connected to your LAN via remote bridges, you should protect the bridge and obtain a UPS system with the capacity to provide extended runtimes for both the file server and bridge. Doing so would enable other network users not affected by the power failure in your building to continue to access data stored on your LAN.

Power protection

Today power protection in many instances is as important as, or more important than, power backup. Indeed, recognizing the fact that varying utility power levels as well as lightening can adversely effect critical electronic components, modern UPS systems include a power conditioning capability.

However, the extent of power conditioning varies between products as well as between products in the same vendor's product line.

Line noise Line noise, more commonly known as electromagnetic interference (EMI) and radio frequency interference (RFI), can result from lightening, generators, radio transmitters and other types of equipment. Line noise results in a displacement of the smooth, repetitive sine wave that electrical equipment expects, causing power variations that can result in the corruption of an executing program.

Voltage sags A voltage sag is a temporary reduction in an expected voltage level. Voltage sags typically result from the start-up power requirements of other electrical equipment, reducing the available voltage.

However, sags also represent the deliberate mechanism by which electrical utilities cope with abnormal power demands in very cold or very warm weather. During those times, utilities lower voltage levels, a condition referred to as a brownout. While this will not adversely affect a toaster, it can reduce the power level necessary for a computer to operate correctly, which can result in the loss or corruption of data.

According to several studies, voltage sags account for the vast majority of power problems at the wall outlet. Power sags account for almost 90% of power problems, followed by voltage spikes and blackouts.

Voltage spikes A voltage spike is a very sharp increase in the level of voltage for a very short period of time. Typically resulting from lightening, voltage spikes are also created after a power disruption when power is initially restored. A voltage spike can literally "fry" computer equipment, causing damage to hardware as well as loss of data.

Voltage surges A voltage surge represents a short-term increase in the voltage level which lasts for a fraction of a second. Here the increase in the level of voltage is considerably less than that of a voltage spike, while the duration considerably exceeds that of a spike.

The primary cause of voltage surges are compressors in air conditioners and other appliances which, when switched off, result in disruption on the power line.

Voltage surges, while typically accounting for less than 1% of power problems, can stress electrical components since electronic devices are designed to receive power within a certain predefined voltage range. Thus, voltage surges can result in equipment failing prematurely.

Power loss A loss of power can result from a variety of problems, ranging from ice on power lines, trees falling across power lines during a storm, to car accidents and the rolling blackout of a utility when demand exceeds available supply. When power is suddenly lost your equipment can be damaged and any work in RAM will be lost. As previously discussed, the original design goal of UPS systems was to compensate for power losses.

UPS features

One could probably list more than 50 items for comparison between vendor's products. However, many items can be placed into a common feature category for initial comparison purposes which would reduce the number of items during your initial comparison of competitive products. Then, once you complete your initial comparison of vendor products you could perform a more detailed analysis of products which survived your initial screening.

Table 5.7 gives 15 general UPS features you may wish to consider when initially comparing different vendor products. In preparing the list, several major groupings of related features were performed. For example, filtering of utility power to include the removal of spikes, transients and other irregularities, as well as EMI and RFI filtering, was replaced by the "Power regulation and protection" entry. Similarly, the "Software configurability" entry can represent numerous individual UPS parameter settings in a network environment, such as setting the time delay prior to the UPS sending a message that it is operating on battery power and the frequency with which subsequent messages are transmitted to network users.

Although most of the entries in Table 5.7 are self-explanatory, a few deserve a degree of elaboration. The "Automatic bypass"

Table 5.7 UPS features to consider.

Audible alarm upon power failure
Automatic bypass
Automatic voltage selection
Backup time at full load
Battery recharge time
Battery replacement warning
Capacity in VA or kVA
Front panel indicators
Mean time before failure
Power regulation and protection
Novell compatibility
SNMP compatibility
Software configurability
Upgradability
Warranty

feature compensates for an internal UPS failure and transfers the load from the UPS back to the utility. Typically, the UPS with this feature includes a temperature sensor and will initiate a bypass operation if the temperature exceeds a predefined value. This feature increases the system reliability of the UPS beyond the typical 30 000 to 40 000 MTBF hours of many products.

The "Automatic voltage selection" feature permits a UPS to be used with different utility power sources, such as 110 and 220 volts. Some vendors add an international automatic voltage source capability which permits 240 volts at 50Hz as well as 110 and 220 volts at 60Hz.

"Novell compatibility" and "SNMP compatibility" permit a UPS to be controlled from any node in a network that can communicate using Novell's IPX or TCP/IP. However, the actual parameters of the UPS you can control would be governed by the software configurability of the UPS system.

Concerning "Upgradability", several UPS vendors now manufacture systems quite similar to the familiar Lego blocks. By adding an extra battery unit or units to a base unit, you expand the capacity and backup time of the overall system. Now that we have background information concerning the general UPS features we may wish to compare, let's turn our attention to UPS network features.

Network features

A number of recently introduced UPS systems can be cabled to Ethernet and Token-Ring networks through the use of Simple Network Management Protocol (SNMP) adapters. Here the adapter is cabled to the network and the UPS is cabled to the adapter. Through the use of appropriate software you can control many UPS functions from a workstation on the network.

For example, on a NetWare LAN you could use the console command UPS STATUS to check the status of the UPS, and UPS TIME to change the amount of time you want to allow the network to function on battery power. With certain third party software used in conjunction with UPS hardware you can extend UPS control. That control extension can include specifying the delay prior to sending messages concerning the operation on backup power, specifying the UPS turnoff and wakeup delay time, the operation of an audible warning, and the display and logging of power events. Concerning the latter, this information can be valuable to provide evidence of power problems to the building manager or electric utility.

Alternatives to UPS

If you cannot afford to place all network equipment on a UPS system, you should consider the use of surge suppressors and power line conditioners. A surge suppressor diverts voltage spikes over an alternative path to minimize damage. However, most surge suppressors can only be used once to protect equipment from a major surge, as they are literally consumed by the diversion process. Since most surge protectors do not indicate that they are no longer operational they may provide a false sense of security. In addition, many surge protectors, especially the low cost surge strips, do not filter out noise. Thus, most network managers should consider either a more expensive surge suppressor with a reset indicator, reset capability and noise filtering capability or the use of a power line conditioner.

Power line conditioners provide protection from spikes and surges as well as from noise. Owing to their greater protection capacity they cost more than simple surge protectors, but in the long term their cost may be warranted if they save equipment.

FILE ACCESS CONTROL

Among numerous threats to data stored on networked computers are intentional or unintentional unauthorized access. One of the keys to preventing unauthorized access is the appropriate use of file access control software.

This chapter will describe a variety of file access control tools and techniques, ranging in scope from different types of rights and permissions to the use of passwords and file encryption. To provide readers with a foundation concerning how software actually controls file access, and why some software provides a false sense of protection, we will first review use of the DOS file attribute byte. This will be followed by an examination of UNIX and NetWare, including the UNIX permission mask and the method by which NetWare supports directory and file security.

Since no system is foolproof, we will briefly discuss the use of file encryption to protect the contents of files from observation, deferring until Chapter 7 a detailed investigation of the use of encryption software and hardware. Even if your network is completely secure you may wish to consider encryption of files prior to transmitting information over communications carrier facilities and E-mail systems, where the contents of your data may be exposed to compromise.

6.1 THE DOS FILE ATTRIBUTE BYTE

Each directory entry on a DOS diskette is 32 bytes long. Of particular interest is byte 11, whose composition indicates the file's attributes. Currently DOS uses six bits within byte 11 of each directory entry, as indicated in Figure 6.1. Of those six bit positions, four can be directly modified through the use of the DOS ATTRIB command. Those bits are the archive, read-only,

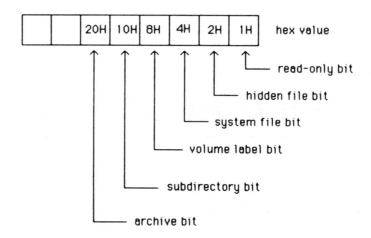

Figure 6.1 Current use of the DOS attribute byte.

system and hidden file bits. The remaining two archive bits, volume label and subdirectory, are set and reset by the operating system based upon the use of the VOL command to create a volume label and MD and RD commands to create and remove subdirectories.

To obtain an appreciation for each bit position in the attribute byte let's first discuss how the bit positions are used. Then we can examine use of the ATTRIB command to set and reset certain bit positions.

Read-only bit

The rightmost bit in the DOS attribute byte indicates whether or not the file is marked as a read-only file. This bit can be set along with other attribute byte bits. When set, it precludes a user from being able to write onto the contents of a file. However, as we will soon note, the ATTRIB command provides an easy mechanism for the removal of the setting of the read-only bit.

Hidden file bit

The next bit position indicates whether or not a file is hidden. When that bit position is set the file is excluded from normal directory searches. As with the read-only bit, the hidden bit can be set and reset through the use of the ATTRIB command. Thus, a hidden file does not provide any real security beyond hiding the file from casual observation.

System file bit

As with the hidden file bit position, setting of the system file bit position excludes the file from normal directory searches. Thus, this bit setting does not provide any real security beyond hiding a file from casual observation.

Volume label bit

The volume label bit is used to indicate that the first 11 bytes in the directory entry represent a volume label. This bit position serves to distinguish normal directory entries from the volume label assigned to a disk.

Subdirectory bit

Although subdirectory entries are contained in a disk directory, they require a mechanism to distinguish them from a file. That mechanism is the subdirectory bit, whose setting indicates that the entry in the directory represents a subdirectory and should be excluded from directory searches.

Archive bit

The last bit currently used in the DOS attribute byte is the archive bit. This bit is set whenever the file is written to and closed. Both the BACKUP and RESTORE commands use the archive bit to determine whether the file was changed since a prior backup operation. The ATTRIB command can be used to set and reset this bit position.

The ATTRIB command

The ATTRIB command provides the ability to easily set and reset four of the DOS attribute byte bit positions—read-only, archive, system and hidden. Prior to DOS 3.3 the ATTRIB command only toggled the read-only attribute of a file. Thus, persons were forced to use third-party utility routines or develop their own program to alter the system, hidden and archive file bits. This resulted in some persons using programs developed to hide files obtaining a false level of security when they hid a file.

Figure 6.2 illustrates, through the DOS help facility, the structure or format of the ATTRIB command, including parameters you can use in the command. To illustrate how the ATTRIB command provides an easy mechanism both to locate files normally hidden from view and to change their attribute byte bit settings, let us use that command.

The top of Figure 6.3 illustrates use of the DIR command to obtain directory information concerning the file GEM.BAT. Next, the middle portion of Figure 6.3 illustrates use of the ATTRIB command with the +h parameter to set the hidden file bit of the file GEM.BAT. A subsequent directory listing in the lower portion of Figure 6.3 indicates that the DIR command cannot locate the file since it is now hidden.

Although the file GEM.BAT was hidden, it was only hidden from normal directory searches. In fact, you can use the ATTRIB command to display the attribute bit settings of a specific file, a group of files, or all files on your disk to include hidden files. For example, entering the command ATTRIB *.* would result in the display of all files in the current directory, including system and hidden files previously hidden from view by the use of the DIR command. Figure 6.4 illustrates use of the ATTRIB com-

---

```
C:\>help attrib
Displays or changes file attributes

ATTRIB [+R | -R] [+A | -A] [+S | - S] [+H | -H]
[[drive:] [path]filename] [/S]

              +      Sets an attribute.
                     Clears an attribute.
              R      Read-only file attribute.
              A      Archive file attribute.
              S      System file attribute.
              H      Hidden file attribute.
              /S     Processes files in all directories in the
                     specified path.
```

Figure 6.2 DOS ATTRIB command format.

```
C:\>dir gem.bat

Volume in drive C has no label
Volume Serial Number is 1A32-61A4
Directory of C:\

GEM          BAT          151 10-27-88  3:10a
             1 file(s)         151 bytes
                          96395264 bytes free

c:\>attrib + h gem.bat

C:\>dir gem.bat

Volume in drive C has no label
volume Serial Number is 1A32=61A4
Directory of C:\

File not found
```

Figure 6.3 Using the ATTRIB command to hide a file.

```
C:\>attrib I*.*
             SH           C:\IO.SYS
    A        SHR          C:\IITV3.VOL
             SHR          C:\IMAGE.IDX
    A        R            C:\IMAGE.DAT
    A        R            C:\IMAGE.BAK
```

Figure 6.4 Using the ATTRIB command to display the attribute bit settings of all files in the current directory whose first letter is "I".

mand to display the attribute bit settings of all files whose filename begin with the letter I, regardless of file extension.

Security modifications

Recognizing the fact that the ATTRIB byte does not actually provide a true file security mechanism, software and hardware developers introduced a number of products designed to compensate for the vulnerability of DOS. Some products provide access control at the physical level, usually consisting of a special adapter card which is inserted into the system unit of the computer. The adapter contains ROM code which bypasses normal BIOS and prompts the user to enter a password to obtain access to the computer. Since normal BIOS is bypassed, a user cannot simply place a diskette containing the operating system in drive A to bypass this access control mechanism. Readers are referred back to Chapter 2 for specific information concerning different types of physical access control.

A second popular access control mechanism developed by numerous third party vendors involves encryption of the contents of a file. Although encryption does not prevent the ability of an unauthorized user to access a file, it precludes that user from accessing the contents of the file in a meaningful manner. Readers are referred to Chapter 7 for specific information concerning the use of encryption software as a mechanism to protect both stored and transmitted information.

6.2 UNIX PERMISSIONS

UNIX is a much more comprehensive and sophisticated operating system than DOS, represented not only by its ability to perform multitasking operations but, in addition, by its more sophisticated access control features.

User names and groups

Multitasking was incorporated into UNIX by design, as this operating system was developed to support groups of programmers who required access to a multiuser computing system. This design resulted in two types of user names being recognized by UNIX—individual user names and user groups.

Each authorized user of a UNIX system is identified to the system by a unique user name that can consist of up to eight characters in length. That name is associated by the operating system with a unique user number referred to as a user-ID, which is used internally within UNIX.

Each UNIX system user can be a member of one or more user groups that are defined to the system. For example, circuit designers, financial analysts and procurement specialists represent three types of job categories that could warrant the establishment of separate groups to facilitate data sharing among group members. Similar to user names, user groups are identified by a name consisting of up to eight characters in length and are associated by the operating system with a unique group-ID number. Each UNIX user can be a member of more than one group, but their membership can be active in only one group at any point in time.

File and directory permissions

Permissions govern which users have the ability to access a file or directory as well as the type of access that is permitted. Under UNIX each file and directory supports read (r), write (w), and execute/search (x) permissions. Those permissions can be set for the owner of a file or directory, a group associated with a file or directory and for all "others" on the system for each file and directory. Access to each file and directory is based upon the user's identification code (UID), their primary group identification code (GID), and the specific permission mask of the file or directory. Thus, the permission mask can be considered as a more sophisticated version of the DOS attribute byte, providing access control to files and directories for both individual as well as for all users of the computer.

Figure 6.5 illustrates the relationship of UNIX permissions for directory and file operations. Once a user is logged into a system, each file and directory operation first results in a comparison of the user's UID with the owner of the file. If they match,

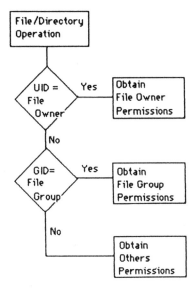

Figure 6.5   Relationship of UNIX permissions.

the user obtains owner permissions. If they do not match, the user's GID is compared with the owner's group. If a match occurs the user obtains group permissions. If the user's GID does not match the owner's group then the user obtains "others" permissions.

The permission mask

A UNIX permission mask is a 9-bit or three-digit octal number constructed through a logical OR operation of all mode settings. Thus, to understand how the permission mask is formed requires a review of each potential permission mask setting. Figure 6.6 shows the UNIX permission mask bit settings for all possible owner, group and "others" file and directory read, write and execute/search permissions. We will use the entries in Figure 6.6 to illustrate how the UNIX permission mask is formed.

Formation

To illustrate the formation of a UNIX file permission mask let us assume a user named Walt owns the file CLINTON.JOK created on 1 April. Further assume that members of the group "admin" were provided permission to read, write and execute/search the file, while all other users are only allowed

Bit settings				Permissions			
Octal	Binary			Owner	Group	Others	Descriptions
400	100	000	000	r--	---	---	Read by owner
200	010	000	000	-w-	---	---	Write by owner
100	001	000	000	--x	---	---	Execute file or search by owner
040	000	100	000	---	r--	---	Read by group
020	000	010	000	---	-w-	---	Write by group
010	000	001	000	---	--x	---	Execute file or search by group
004	000	000	100	---	---	r--	Read by others
002	000	000	010	---	---	-w-	Write by others
001	000	000	001	---	---	--x	Execute file or search by others

Figure 6.6 UNIX permission mask bit settings.

to read the file. Thus, the owner will have "rwx" permissions, the group will have "rwx" permissions, while all "other" users on the system will have "r" permission to the file (see Figure 6.7) illustrates the creation of the p-ermission mask for the file CLIN-TON.JOK.

The resulting permission mask will have the value 774 octal which represents the summed value of all allowable per-missions. If you used the UNIX ls command with the -l (long) option to display information about the file CLINTON.JOK, you would have the following line displayed on your monitor:

```
-rwxrwxr-- 1 walt  admin 1298 Apr 1 12:00 clinton.jok
```

In the above line listing, the entries "walt" and "admin" rep-resent the owner "walt" and group "admin" associated with the file, while 1298 represents its file size in bytes. The numeric 1 before walt denotes the number of links to the file, a term used to indicate how many names the file is known by.

Directory permissions

Permission masks are also applicable to directories. The key dif-ference between the application of permission masks to files and to directories concerns the operations allowed by each per-mission and the manner in which the permission mask is dis-

| Bit settings | | | | Permissions | | | |
Octal	Binary			Owner	Group	Others	Descriptions
400	100	000	000	r--	---	---	Read by owner
200	010	000	000	-w-	---	---	Write by owner
100	001	000	000	--x	---	---	Execute file or search by owner
040	000	100	000	---	r--	---	Read by group
020	000	010	000	---	-w-	---	Write by group
010	000	001	000	---	--x	---	Execute file or search by group
004	000	000	100	---	---	r--	Read by others
744	111	111	100	rwx	rwx	r--	Permission mask

Figure 6.7 Formation of the UNIX file permission mask.

played. Table 6.1 compares the applicability of r, w and x permissions to files and directories under UNIX.

If the file permission mask created in Figure 6.7 was applied to a directory named Willie owned by user "walt" and group "admin", this mask would allow the user walt to use the CD command to change to the directory named Willie, list its contents, and create, modify, delete and rename files in that directory. Members of the group "admin" would have the same capability based upon the permission assigned in Figure 6.7, while all other users would have only the ability to use the CD command to change to the directory Willie and list files in that directory.

To differentiate between the permission masks of files and directories, use of the LS command results in the letter "d" prefixing the permission mask when the mask is associated with a directory. Now that we have an understanding of the file and directory permission masks let's focus our attention upon how the mask is created and modified.

Mask manipulation

When a file or directory is created from the UNIX command line a default permission is assigned. That permission is 666 octal for files and 777 octal for directories. This results in read and

Table 6.1 UNIX file and directory permission comparison.

Permission	File	Directory
r	Permits display of the contents of a file and copying of the file	Permits listing of the contents of a directory
w	Permits a file to be modified or deleted	Permits files and subdirectories in the directory to be created, modified, deleted or renamed if permissions on existing files and subdirectories permit those operations
x	Permits a file represented by a compiled program or shell script to be executed	Permits the CD command to be used to change to a directory and the LS command to be used to list files in the directory

write permissions for the owner, group and "others" for files, while read, write and execute permissions are applicable for directories.

When a file or directory is created by a program, the program normally governs the permissions associated with the files or directories. The exception to this occurs through the use of the UNMASK (userfile creation mask) command. That command can be used by a user to modify the permissions for newly created files and directories created by a program or through a command line entry.

UNMASK command

The format of the UNMASK command is "unmask [value]". If no value is used in the command, the command simply displays the current unmask value, while the inclusion of a value resets the unmask value to that specified.

The unmask value is subtracted from the default file or directory permission, which results in the actual permission assigned to the file or directory.

The default unmask value is 000 octal which does not reduce any permissions from the permission mask. When the UNMASK command is used to set the unmask value to a setting other than 000 octal, this results in a reduction in the permission settings of a file or directory. For example, to deny the group and "others" the ability to have write permission for newly created files and directories, you would use an unmask value of 022 octal. Then, when a file is created the unmask value of 022 octal is subtracted from its default permission of 666 octal. Thus, 666 – 022 is 644, which represents the permission mask - rw-r--r--. For a directory which has a default permission of 777 octal, the subtraction of the unmask value of 022 octal results in a permission mask of 755 octal. That value results in a permission mask of drwxr-xr-x.

We can summarize UNIX file and directory permissions to file and directory tasks. This summary is contained in Table 6.2 and summarizes the permissions required to perform file and directory tasks in a UNIX environment. One entry requires a degree of elaboration. That entry is the directory permissions to read the contents of a file.

If the directory permissions does not include the "r" permission, a user cannot list the names of files in the directory.

Table 6.2 UNIX file and directory permission tasks.

Task	Permissions file	Required directory
Read contents of a file	r	rx
Copy a file from a directory	r	x
Modify a file in a directory	rw	wx
Delete a file in a directory	–	wx
Execute a file	x	x
List files in a directory	–	rx
Create a file in a directory	–	wx
Rename a file in a directory	r	wx
CD to a directory	–	x

However, if the user knows or can guess the name of a file and has read permission for the file, he or she can read the contents of the file.

Another use of the entries in Table 6.2 is that they illustrate some basic concepts and guidelines that are highly recommended for readers to follow when assigning UNIX permissions. First, without providing both "rw" permissions to a file and "wx" permissions to the directory in which a file resides the file cannot be modified. Secondly, if a file does not have "w" permission but the directory in which it resides has "wx" permissions, the protection for the file can be overwritten and the file can be removed.

Permission manipulation

UNIX supports several commands which enable users to directly and indirectly change permissions associated with a file. One command, CHMOD, permits the file owner or supervisor to change permissions associated with a file. Another command, CHOWN, is only applicable for use by the supervisor and enables that person to change the ownership of a file. A third command, CHGRP, performs the same function for the group that owns a file.

The supervisor The term "supervisor" refers to the person who has the ability to perform system administration functions. By convention, the supervisor is given the user name "root" and becomes the owner of the root directory which is located at the top of the hierarchical directory structure supported by the operating system. The supervisor is also the owner of other key UNIX files and directories, such as the operating system kernel. This provides the supervisor with the ability to authorize new users, abolish existing users, and perform other administrative functions. To provide the supervisor with the power to perform such functions, all UNIX permissions and protection mechanisms are bypassed for this powerful user. Thus, the user name "root" should always be password-protected to preserve the integrity of the system.

One common potential supervisor security breach is the fact that every system is initially setup to recognize a default password. Although it should be obvious that this password should be changed, one can read many "horror stories" which tell of situations in which the authorized supervisor continued to use the default password until the system was retired or a security problem caused the supervisor to retire.

CHOWN and CHGRP utilities CHOWN, an acronym for change owner, provides the supervisor with the ability to change the ownership of a file. The format of this command is:

```
chown [newowner] [filename]
```

An example is "chown fred pay.dat", which would result in the user named Fred becoming the owner of the file PAY.DAT.

CHGRP, an acronym for change group, enables a change in the group owner of a file. The format of that command is:

```
chgrp [newgroup] [filename]
```

An example is "chgrp engr circuit.test", which would result in the group named "engr" becoming the owner of the file CIRCUIT.TEST.

CHMOD utility CHMOD, an acronym for change mode, permits the supervisor to change each of the nine permissions associated with a file or directory. This command supports the use of octal digits or alphabetic characters to specify the granting or restricting of permissions to the owner, group or "others".

For example, "chmod +rw pay.dat" would grant read and write access to all three classes of users to the file PAY.DAT, while the command "chmod g –w pay.dat" would deny write access to users in the group owning the file.

Table 6.3 lists the octal values for the allowable permissions in a CHMOD command. Each command would have three octal digits, with the leftmost representing owner permissions, the middle representing group permissions and the right octal digit representing "other" permissions.

As an example of the use of the entries in Table 6.3, consider the command "chmod 774 pay.txt". This command would provide read, write and execute permissions to the owner and group members for the file PAY.TXT. However, all "others" users would be restricted to read access to that file.

Directory structure

UNIX, like DOS, supports a hierarchical directory structure with the root at the top of the structure. This is used by UNIX to organize its system files, and the operating system uses certain directory locations to store predefined files. By reviewing a portion of the UNIX directory structure, we can note some potential security vulnerabilities as well as discuss actions we can consider to reduce those vulnerabilities.

Figure 6.8 illustrates the standard UNIX directory structure. Under the USR directory, organizations typically add individual user directories as well as directories whose contents may be shared by other users and user groups. The directory structure illustrated can be considered to represent a model, to which many organizations add directories and subdirectories to tailor

Table 6.3 CHMOD permissions.

Value	Permission
0	No access
1	Execute access
2	Write access
3	Write and execute access
4	Read access
5	Read and execute access
6	Read and write access
7	Read, write and execute access

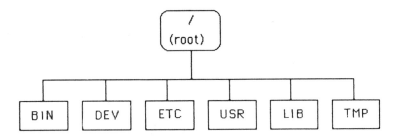

Figure 6.8 Basic UNIX directory structure.

the structure to their specific processing requirements. Later in this section we will discuss the use of a directory appropriately labeled "incoming" as a repository for receiving information from users outside the immediate organization.

The BIN directory is used to store UNIX utilities, while the DEV directory is used to store special files, such as I/O devices. The USR directory will normally have subdirectories for each user of the system and results in a nested directory structure. The LIB directory typically contains libraries used by the UNIX language processors, while TMP, as its abbreviation implies, is normally a repository for temporary files.

The ETC directory

Perhaps one of the most important directories from a security perspective is ETC, which is used to contain administrative programs and tables. The system administrator will maintain a list of authorized users as well as other important user information in the file PASSWD which is located in the ETC directory. Similarly, information about groups and group membership is placed in the file group which is also located in the ETC directory.

You can facilitate system security by making the owner of the ETC subdirectory the owner of the root and restrict write permission to ETC, so that only the root owner can do so. This action will prevent other users from being able to modify important files that govern access to the system.

If a UNIX system is connected to a modem to provide dial-in access or to the Internet, there are several actions you can consider to minimize the potential exposure of your computer to unwanted software, such as bootlegged copyrighted software or a hidden virus. To control incoming software you should set up a special directory limited to a "wx" permission. Many systems do so and appropriately name that directory "incoming", which explains why you cannot list the files in that directory. In controlling that directory, you should limit both the amount of data that can be uploaded into INCOMING during one session as well as the maximum amount of data that can be stored in the directory. Doing so will prevent a system from being maliciously filled with jokes or other unwanted material in an attempt to hog resources which can deny service to legitimate users. On a periodic basis, the files added to the directory INCOMING should be reviewed both for applicability for placement into an appropriate directory on your system as well as for the inclusion of attack software. (Readers are referred back to Chapter 5 for specific information concerning attack software.)

One common alternative to the use of "wx" permission for an INCOMING directory concerns the use of that directory on an anonymous FTP server connected to the Internet. Many anonymous FTP sites establish their directory structure so that the FTP root directory and its subdirectories are owned by the root. This results in only the root having write permission to each directory.

Figure 6.9 illustrates the results of a directory listing once a connection to the Internet address FTP.SURA.NET was estab-

```
Command:
dir
>>>PORT 198,78,46,1,5,160
200 PORT command successful.
>>>LIST
150 Opening ASCII mode data connection for /bin/ls.
total 24
drwxrwx--x      3  0   0      512 Jun 22 1993   bin
drwxr-xr-x      2  0   1      512 Dec 7  04:12 etc
drwxrwx--x      6  0   10     512 Feb 28 21:52 incoming
drwxr-xr-x      2  0   0     8192 Feb 15 1992   lost+found
drwxrwxr-x     21  0   100    512 Feb 10 21:54 pub
226 Transfer complete.

Command:
cd incoming
>>>CWD incoming
250 CWD command successful.
```

Figure 6.9 Examining directory permissions on an anonymous FTP server.

lished. That address represents the anonymous FTP server of SuraNet, an Internet access provider located in the south-east United States. Note that only the owner has full permissions for each directory. Also note that "others", which represent all persons accessing the server as an anonymous user, lack write permission to every directory, precluding the alteration of information by that user category.

Since an "x" permission enables an anonymous user to use the CD command to change to the INCOMING directory, some anonymous FTP sites create subdirectories in the FTP/INCOMING directory using names known to anonymous users the site administrator wants to have "drop off" permission. For example, a supervisor might create the subdirectory ETGOHOME. That would have permissions "rwxrwx-wx", permitting anonymous users that know they should CD to ETGOHOME the ability to drop off information into that directory.

6.3 NETWARE

Under NetWare the concept and operation of file access control is considerably expanded. In addition to supporting the assignment of eight rights to directories and files, NetWare also supports the use of trustee rights which govern the ability of an individual user or group to access directories and work with their contents. Since an understanding of file access control requires an understanding of the rights supported by NetWare, those rights represent a good starting point for a review of the file access control features of this network operating system.

Rights

NetWare supports eight types of rights which individually and collectively control the directories and files a user or group of users can access and the operations they can perform. Table 6.4 lists the rights supported by NetWare as well as a brief description of the effect of each right.

While most of the entries in Table 6.4 are self-explanatory, two warrant a bit of elaboration for those readers not intimately knowledgeable about NetWare. The first right which requires a degree of elaboration is the Create right, which when applied to

Table 6.4   NetWare directory and file rights.

Right	Mnemonic	Description
Supervisor	S	All rights to a file or directory
Read	R	Enables users to open and read files
Write	W	Allows users to write to files
Create	C	Enables users to create directories and salvage a file after it is deleted
Erase	E	Allows users to delete files and directories
Modify	M	Enables users to change directories and file attributes as well as rename directories and files
Scan	F	Enables users to see files and subdirectories in a directory
Access	A	Allows users to change access control

files permits a user to salvage a file after it is deleted. Under NetWare 3.11 and later versions of this operating system, the system can be configured to save deleted files automatically in a directory named DELETED.SAV, located under the root directory. Each deleted file will remain in that directory until the user purges the file or until the server runs out of allocated space for deleted files and automatically purges those files on a first deleted, first purged basis. Thus, the Create right provides a user with the ability to recover a file after it was deleted.

The second right which requires elaboration is Access. This right, when assigned, enables users to modify trustee assignments and what is known as the Inherited Rights Mask (IRM). A trustee is a user or group that was assigned rights to work in a directory or use a file.

Under NetWare, access control is primarily based upon trustee rights, which specify who has specific rights to files and directories. The Inherited Rights Mask is assigned to each file when it is created and controls which rights users can inherit. The default IRM includes all NetWare rights listed in Table 6.4. However, users may not be able to exercise all of those rights since trustee assignments serve as a filter which controls the effective rights a user obtains. Later in this section we will examine several examples of the use of trustee rights and the IRM, as well as the resulting effective rights.

The RIGHTS command

To determine the rights associated with a directory or file you can use the RIGHTS command. Figure 6.10 illustrates its use to determine the rights associated with the file FRED.USR.

Note that NetWare displays the effective rights for directories and files in the form of up to eight alphabetic characters contained in brackets in a horizontal row, with the omission of a character indicating that that right is not provided.

Effective rights

The actual rights a user can exercise in a directory or file are referred to as the "effective rights" of the directory or file. A user's effective rights are based upon the rights granted in a trustee assignment for the user and any groups the user belongs to, as well as the rights in the Inherited Rights Mask. Thus, let us first focus our attention upon trustee rights and the IRM prior to discussing the formation of a user's effective rights.

Trustee rights A trustee is a user or group assigned one or more rights to enable the use of a directory and files within a directory. Once a user or group has been assigned rights to work in a directory or file, they then become the "trustee" of the directory.

```
F:\USERS\GXHELD)rights fred.usr
MDPC-1\SYS:USERS\GXHELD\FRED.USR
Your Effective Rights for this file are        [SRWCEMFA]
        You have Supervisor Rights to File.        (S)
        May Read from File.                        (R)
        May Write to File.                         (W)
  *     May Create Subdirectories and Files.       (C)
        May Erase File.                            (E)
        May Modify File.                           (M)
        May Scan for File.                         (F)
        May Change Access Control                  (A)

  *  Create is necessary to salvage a file that has been deleted.

     You have ALL RIGHTS to Directory Entry.
```

Figure 6.10 Using the RIGHTS command.

The assignment of trustee rights is accomplished by the network supervisor through use of the NetWare SYSCON (system console) utility program. Figure 6.11 illustrates the display of trustee rights granted to user Fred to the directory USERS/FRED, accomplished by moving the highlight bar over the entry SYS:USERS/FRED in the window labeled "Trustee Directory Assignments" and pressing the Enter key. In fact, by selecting the Trustee Directory Assignment entry in the SYSCON User Information window all trustee directory assignments for the specified user name are displayed. However, that display, which is shown in the upper right portion of the window labeled "Trustee Directory Assignments", lists the rights in brackets in their abbreviated NetWare notation form. By selecting a directory and pressing the Enter key, the resulting window labeled "Trustee Rights Granted", which is displayed in the left portion of Figure 6.11, fully describes the rights granted. That window also provides you with the ability to remove or revoke previously granted rights.

By moving the highlight bar over an appropriate right and pressing the Delete key, the window labeled "Revoke Trustee Right" is displayed in the center of the screen, providing the

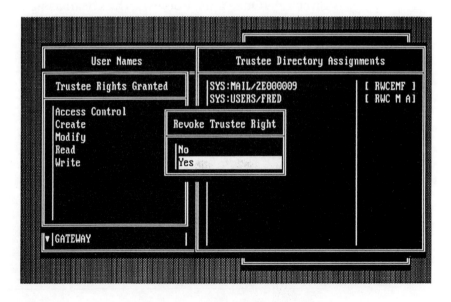

Figure 6.11 Using SYSCON to revoke a right.

supervisor with the ability to delete a right. If you press the Insert key when the highlight bar is located in the "Trustee Rights Granted" window, a new window labeled "Trustee Rights Not Granted" is displayed in the right portion of the screen. This is illustrated in Figure 6.12. By moving the highlight bar over a right not granted and pressing the Enter key, the supervisor can grant a right.

Inherited rights mask As its name implies, an Inherited Rights Mask or IRM are the rights provided to a file or directory when they are created. The default IRM includes all rights, but the actual rights in an IRM are initially based upon the rights granted in a trustee assignment. Those rights can be modified through the use of the ALLOW command which can also be used to view the currently assigned IRM. By modifying the IRM you can restrict the inherited rights to subdirectories and files.

Figure 6.13 illustrates use of the ALLOW command after a directory listing indicates the presence of the file PAY.DAT in the directory FRED. Note that the format of the command is "allow [filename] [rightslist]" where the rights in the [rightslist]

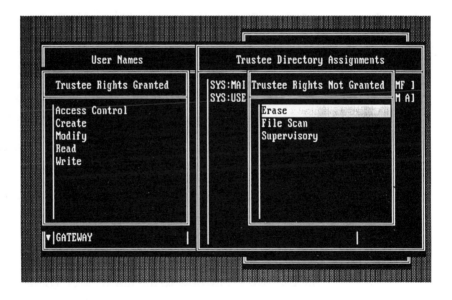

Figure 6.12 Using SYSCON to grant a right.

```
:\USERS\FRED)dir

Volume in drive F is SYS
Volume Serial Number is D8FF-7CD9
Directory of F:\USERS\FRED

AY           DAT      366 03-03-94 1:47p
             1 file(s)      366    bytes
                       64421888 bytes free

:\USERS\FRED)allow pay.dat
   Files:
      PAY.DAT                              [SRWCEMFA]

:\USERS\FRED)allow pay.dat r w c
   Files:
      PAY.DAT
                                           [WRWC    ]
```

Figure 6.13 Using the ALLOW command to display and change the rights associated with a file.

form the rights assigned to the file. Hence, the command ALLOW PAY.DAT displays the rights of the file, while the command ALLOW PAY.DAT R W C sets the rights Read, Write and Create to the file.

To change the Inherited Rights Mask for a directory, the supervisor or a person with supervisory rights can use the NetWare FILER utility program. Figure 6.14 illustrates the use of FILER to review the IRM assigned to the directory FRED. On moving the highlight bar over the IRM and pressing the Return key, the FILER utility program will display the inherited rights. You can then move a highlight bar over a right you wish to revoke and press the Delete key. This action causes FILER to prompt you to verify your action, as illustrated in Figure 6.15.

As indicated in Figure 6.14, you can also use FILER to view the trustees of a directory. Once you do so, you can also use FILER to change trustee rights. This is illustrated in Figure 6.16, which displays the trustee rights assigned to the directory FRED. As with most NetWare utilities, by moving the highlight bar over an appropriate entry and pressing either the Insert or Delete key you can assign or revoke a previously selected right. Now that we know how to assign trustee rights and manipulate the IRM let's return our attention to the focus of this section, which is the formation of the effective rights.

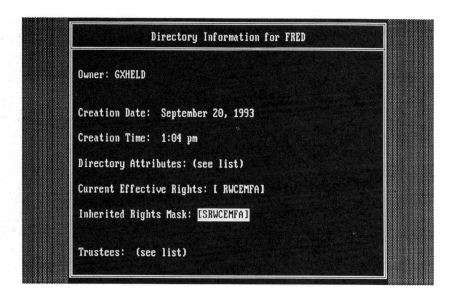

```
┌────────────────────────────────────────────────┐
│           Directory Information for FRED          │
├────────────────────────────────────────────────┤
│  Owner: GXHELD                                    │
│                                                   │
│  Creation Date:  September 20, 1993               │
│                                                   │
│  Creation Time:  1:04 pm                          │
│                                                   │
│  Directory Attributes: (see list)                 │
│                                                   │
│  Current Effective Rights: [ RWCEMFA]             │
│                                                   │
│  Inherited Rights Mask: [SRWCEMFA]                │
│                                                   │
│                                                   │
│  Trustees:  (see list)                            │
└────────────────────────────────────────────────┘
```

Figure 6.14 Using the FILER utility to observe the IRM of a directory.

Directory rights formation

Effective rights are rights a user can actually exercise in a given directory or file. Thus, effective rights can be considered as an important method for controlling the use of programs and distribution of information in a NetWare environment.

The formation of effective rights for a directory can occur by one of two methods. First, the effective rights in a parent directory are determined. Those rights are then modified by the IRM to provide the rights to the subdirectory. A second method involves the granting of a trustee assignment to a directory which overrides the IRM.

The effective rights of a user to a particular directory or file can be expressed through the use of two equations. Normally the effective rights are determined as follows:

Effective rights   *logical*   Inherited
                                                              Rights Mask
of user in parent directory   *AND*

If a new trustee assignment was made to a directory or file,

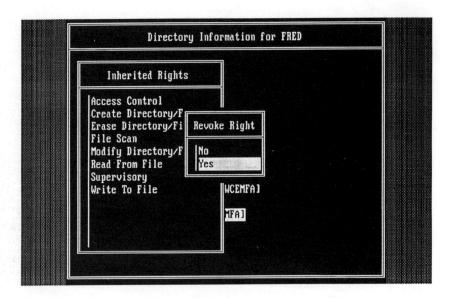

Figure 6.15 Using FILER to revoke a right.

the assignment overrides the IRM and the effective rights from the parent directory. Then, the effective rights of a user in a directory or file are determined as follows:

User trustee assignment	*logical OR*	Trustee assignment for group(s) user belongs to

To illustrate the formation of effective rights, let us work a few examples. First, let us assume we have the Novell directory structure PAYROLL\MONTH. Further assume that the IRM for the directory PAYROLL is [SRWCEMFA], while your trustee assignment rights are [RWCEMF]. Then, your effective rights in the directory PAYROLL become [RWCEMF] as indicated in the upper portion of Figure 6.17. Those effective rights for the parent directory are then filtered by the IRM for the subdirectory. If the IRM for the subdirectory MONTH consisted of all eight rights, then your effective rights in the subdirectory would be the same as your effective rights in the parent directory.

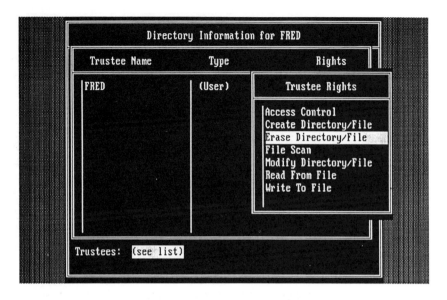

Figure 6.16 Using FILER to view the trustees of a directory and change trustee rights.

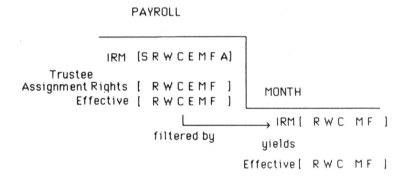

Figure 6.17 Determining the effective rights of a directory.

Now assume that the IRM of the subdirectory is modified by the supervisor, who revokes the S, E and A rights. Then, your effective rights in the subdirectory would be [RWC MF] as illustrated in the lower portion of Figure 6.17. In this example note that a logical AND operation between the effective rights in the parent directory and the IRM was used to obtain the effective rights in the subdirectory.

One of the more interesting features of NetWare is the fact

IRM [RWC MF]
group FINANCE [R E F]
Fred's trustee assignment [WC M]

Fred's effective rights [RWCEMF]

Figure 6.18 Using trustee assignments to modify a user's effective rights.

that trustee assignment rights of a user and a group that the user is a member of are cumulative for directory and file access purposes. For example, assume the user Fred has trustee assignment rights W, C and M to the directory MONTH, while the group Finance, of which he is a member, has R, E and F rights to that directory. Assuming the current IRM is as illustrated in Figure 6.17, Fred's effective rights are computed as illustrated in Figure 6.18. Note that in this example the trustee assignment rights R, E and F of the group Finance are added to Fred's trustee assignment rights to form his effective rights.

If a user is granted supervisory rights to a directory, that user has full rights to all subdirectories under that directory, regardless of the composition of the IRM and any trustee assignment rights. This explains why the network administrator must be very careful in granting supervisory rights to other network users.

File rights formation

The calculation of file effective rights is similar to that described for directory effective rights. Instead of first determining the effective rights of a parent directory, NetWare determines the rights in the directory in which the file is located. In doing so NetWare considers the directory's IRM, a user's trustee assignment rights to the directory, if any, and any group trustee assignment rights to the directory for the user's applicable membership in a group.

To illustrate this, let us work an example. Assume the file CASH.$$$ is located in the directory MONTH whose IRM is [RWCEMFA]. Then, if no trustee assignments are granted for the file, the user's effective rights are the effective rights of the directory in which the file is located. This is illustrated in Figure 6.19.

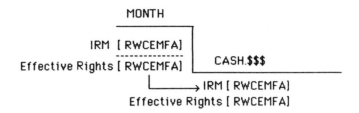

Figure 6.19 Forming a file's effective rights.

Now assume Fred has trustee assignment rights R, W, C, E and M to the directory MONTH. Further assume that the file's IRM was modified by revoking some of its rights, so that it now has the rights R, W and F. Then, Figure 6.20 illustrates the formation of the effective rights for the file CASH.$$$.

In examining Figure 6.20, note that to calculate the file rights first requires the user's effective rights in the parent directory to be determined. In this example, Fred's effective rights in the directory MONTH are R, W, C, E and M. Since the directory rights must be matched with the rights in a file's IRM, the effective rights for the file become R and W.

The effective rights of the parent directory of a file and the file's IRM can be overridden by the granting of a trustee assignment to a file. Then, the user's effective rights become those rights granted in the user and any group trustee assignments. An example of this situation is illustrated in Figure 6.21. In this example, although the IRM for the file has all rights, Fred's trustee assignment rights are limited to R and W. Thus, his effective rights to the file are R and W.

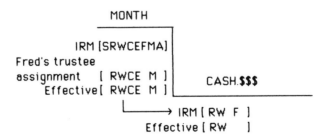

Figure 6.20 Determining a file's effective rights when a trustee assignment modifies the rights of a parent directory.

File CASH:$$$	
IRM	[SRWCEMFA]
Fred's trustee assignment	[RW]
Effective rights	[RW]

Figure 6.21 Trustee assignments to a file override the effective rights of a parent directory and become the file's effective rights.

File and directory attributes

NetWare supports the association of a group of attributes to directories and files. Those attributes are much more powerful than DOS attributes, as their use is more closely embedded within the operating system and can override rights granted with trustee assignments as well as prevent tasks that effective rights would otherwise enable. The attributes associated with a file or directory are often referred to as "attribute security", since the use of attributes can prevent the viewing or deletion of a file or directory, writing to or copying from a file, as well as other functions. The file and directory attributes supported by Net-Ware are summarized in Table 6.5.

Directory and file attributes are displayed by NetWare utilities similarly to the display of rights. That is, the letters of set attributes are displayed between brackets with either spaces or dashes used to indicate attributes that have not been assigned.

Now that we have reviewed the types of attributes that can be associated with files and directories, let us briefly review their functions.

Archive Needed The Archive Needed attribute is automatically assigned to each file modified after a backup. This attribute functions in the same manner as the DOS attribute bit.

Copy Inhibit This attribute is only applicable to users logged onto a NetWare network from a Macintosh workstation. When this attribute is associated with a file, the user logged into the network cannot copy the file. However, if a user was granted the Modify right they could remove the Copy Inhibit attribute and copy the file. Thus, care must be taken when granting a user a Modify right if you do not want the user to copy a particular file.

Table 6.5 Directory and file attributes.

Abbreviation	Description	Applicability (D)irectory	(F)ile
NetWare 3.x			
A	Archive Needed		F
C	Copy Inhibit		F
D	Delete Inhibit	D	F
X	Execute Only		F
H	Hidden	D	F
I	Indexed		F
P	Purge	D	F
Ra	Read Audit		F
Ro/Rw	Read Only/Read		F
R	Rename Inhibit	D	F
S	Shareable		F
Sy	System	D	F
T	Transactional		F
Wa	Write Audit		F
Added to NetWare 4.x			
Co	Compress		F
Cc	Can't Compress		F
Dc	Don't Compress	D	F
Ic	Immediate Compress	D	F
M	Migrated		F
Dm	Don't Migrate	D	F

Delete Inhibit This attribute overrides the Erase right. Thus, when associated with a file or directory the file or directory cannot be erased. However, if a user was granted the Modify right they could remove the Delete Inhibit attribute and delete the directory or file.

Execute Only This attribute precludes the copying of files and can only be assigned by the supervisor or a person with supervisory rights. Care should be used in assigning this attribute as once assigned the attribute cannot be removed.

Hidden This attribute hides a directory or file from a directory listing. In addition, it also prevents a file from being copied or deleted.

Indexed If a file requires more than 64 file entries, NetWare automatically assigns the Indexed attribute to the file and indexes the file. This enables information to be retrieved faster from large files.

Purge   When the Purge attribute is assigned to a file, it is purged when it is deleted. When this attribute is assigned to a directory, NetWare will purge all files in the directory when they are deleted.

Read Audit   This attribute is only applicable to older versions of NetWare. Thus, most versions of NetWare will display a dash or space for the position in which this identifier is located when using a NetWare utility to display file permissions.

Read Only   The assignment of the Ro attribute results in the automatic assignment of Delete Inhibit and Rename Inhibit attributes to a file. Thus, you cannot write to, erase, or rename the file even if you have Write or Erase rights at the directory or file level. However, if you have the Modify right, you can remove the Read Only attribute and write onto, rename, or erase the file.

Rename Inhibit   The Rename Inhibit restricts users from renaming directories and files. However, as with other attributes, if you have the Modify right you can remove this attribute and then rename a directory or file.

Shareable   This attribute permits a file to be used by more than one user at a time. Normally this attribute is used with the Read Only attribute.

System   The System attribute hides files and directories from the DIR command listing, as well as prevents files and directories from being copied or deleted.

Transactional   Assignment of the Transactional attribute results in a file being protected by NetWare's Transactional Tracking System (TTS). TTS protects files from data corruption by ensuring that either all changes to the file or no changes to the file are made when a file is modified.

Write Audit   As with Read Audit, Write Audit is only applicable to versions of NetWare prior to version 3.11. Thus, for most NetWare users a dash or space will be displayed in the Write Audit attribute position when a NetWare utility is used to display the attributes of a file.

NetWare 4.x attribute additions

The introduction of NetWare version 4.0 added six new attributes to the network operating system. The Compress (Co) attribute indicates that a file is compressed, while the Can't Compress (Cc) attribute indicates that a file cannot be compressed since doing so would result in limited space savings.

Two further compression-related attributes added under NetWare 4.0 are Don't Compress (Dc) and Immediate Compress (Ic). Don't Compress is applicable to both files and directories. When assigned to a directory it precludes all files in the directory from being compressed. When added to a specific file it precludes the file from being compressed. The Immediate Compress attribute is also applicable to both directories and files. When added to a directory it alerts the file system to compress all files in the directory as soon as the network operating system can process the request. When the attribute is assigned to a specific file it alerts the file system to compress the file.

The last two attribute additions under NetWare 4.0 are Migrated (M) and Don't Migrate (Dm). The Migrate attribute when set indicates that a specific file was migrated. The Don't Migrate attribute is applicable to both directories and files and its setting precludes all files within a directory or specific files from being migrated to secondary storage.

Attribute manipulation

You can display and change attributes by use of the FILER menu utility and the FLAG and FLAGDIR commands. Since we previously used the FILER utility with rights, let us now examine use of the FLAG and FLAGDIR commands.

The FLAG command can be used to display or change the attributes associated with a file. The format of the command is:

```
flag [filename] [attribute list]
```

Figure 6.22 illustrates three examples of the use of the FLAG command under NetWare 3.1. First the command FLAG *.BAT was used to display the attributes of all files with the extension BAT in the current directory. Since the Purge attribute was not set in any file, the command FLAG MSM.BAT P was entered to illustrate how we can set an attribute to a file, in this example the Purge attribute. The third example shows how to remove a previously set attribute by prefixing the attribute with a minus sign.

The FLAGDIR command functions in a similar manner but is only applicable to directories. In addition to supporting directory names you can use the period (.) in the command to set one or more attributes to the current directory. For example, entering FLAGDIR .R would set the Rename Inhibit attribute to the current directory.

Cautionary postscript

When assigning rights and attributes to files and directories there are several important aspects associated with the structure of NetWare you must consider.

```
F:\USERS\GXHELD)cd\public

F:\PUBLIC)flag *.bat

            MENU.BAT        [ Rw - A - - - - - - - - -- -- -- ]
            XR.BAT          [ Rw S A - - - - - - - - -- -- -- ]
            QUERY.BAT       [ Rw - A - - - - - - - - -- -- -- ]
            MSM.BAT         [ Rw - A - - - - - - - - -- -- -- ]
            NWX.BAT         [ Rw S A - - - - - - - - -- -- -- ]
            NWY1.BAT        [ Rw S A - - - - - - - - -- -- -- ]
            NWX1.BAT        [ Rw S A - - - - - - - - -- -- -- ]
            NWSETUP.BAT     [ Rw S A - - - - - - - - -- -- -- ]
            NWY.BAT         [ Rw S A - - - - - - - - -- -- -- ]
            NWZ.BAT         [ Rw S A - - - - - - - - -- -- -- ]
            NWN.BAT         [ Rw S A - - - - - - - - -- -- -- ]
            NWTECH.BAT      [ Rw S A - - - - - - - - -- -- -- ]

F:\PUBLIC)flag msm.bat p
    MSM.BAT                 [ Rw - A - - - - P -- -- -- -- ]

F:\PUBLIC)flag msm.bat -p
    MSM.BAT                 [ Rw - A - - - - - - - - -- -- ]
```

Figure 6.22 Using the NetWare FLAG command to display, set and reset file attributes.

First, the granting of supervisory rights results in the user or group obtaining all rights, including Modify rights. This means that such users and members of a group with supervisory rights can override such important attributes as Copy Inhibit, Delete Inhibit, Read Only, and Rename Inhibit.

Secondly, granting of the Modify right itself permits override of the previously mentioned attributes. Thus, granting of this right should also be well thought out.

Last but not least, certain attributes can be used to override rights and must also be set with caution. For example, the Delete Inhibit attribute overrides the Erase right.

By understanding the operation and utilization of rights and attributes, you can prevent a breakdown in file and directory protection that could result in the inadvertent or intentional modification or removal of data.

7

TRANSMISSION SECURITY

In examining transmission security, we must consider both intra-LAN and inter-LAN communications as well as remote access to LAN facilities from persons working at home or traveling. The actual protection of data is but one of several factors we must consider. Other areas of concern include verification of the identity of the person who originated a message or transferred a file, and knowledge that the contents of the message or file were not altered. Verification of the identity of a message originator is referred to as "authentication", while a digital "signature" provides a mechanism to both verify the originator of data as well as the fact that the contents of a message or file were not altered.

Owing to the importance of authentication we will examine this topic first. Next, we will discuss several types of *encryption*, including the use of private and public key systems, and how encryption can be used to provide a digital signature, which both verifies the originator of data as well as the authenticity of a transmitted message or file. This information will be used to discuss the operation and utilization of hardware and software products that can be used to provide different levels of transmission security.

7.1 AUTHENTICATION

Authentication refers to the process of verifying the identity of a user, a computer system, or a process, such as the transfer of an electronic mail message. The rationale for authentication can be traced to the growth in decentralized computing, in which terminals previously connected to a computer within a controlled access area began to be relocated, first within the building where the computer was located and later, through the use of communications facilities, to essentially any location in the world.

Passwords

The earliest type of authentication was based upon the use of a password associated with a user ID. Problems with this authentication mechanism arise from the composition and length of the password, which governs its potential for duplication by a third party on a trial and error basis, its distribution, its lifetime prior to change, and the method by which users store their password. Here the composition of the password refers to the character set from which password characters may be used. Obviously, an alphanumeric alphabet set which provides 36 possible characters (if only uppercase letters are considered) provides a higher level of security than a numeric character set.

The length of the password further affects its ability to be compromised. For example, a two-character password based upon the use of numerics has 10^2 or 100 possible combinations. In comparison, a three-character password which supports alphanumeric characters has 36^3 or 46 656 combinations.

Tokens

A second method of authentication involves the use of tokens as discussed in Chapter 2. Here the token value when entered and verified serves to prove the identity of the user who was assigned a token by a token generator.

Tokens were first used as a mechanism to verify the identity of a person accessing mainframe and minicomputers. Later, the use of tokens was expanded to LAN access, both from workstations located on the network as well as from remote users dialing into a LAN to obtain access to local area network facilities.

The use of tokens evolved from an alternative or supplement to the use of passwords associated with user IDs to an access control mechanism to a LAN via remote communications. Concerning the latter, you can now obtain security modems that provide dial-in access to network facilities after a user enters his or her token number, which is verified by the modem communicating with a security server which keeps track of changing token values. Later in this chapter we will discuss the use of security modems to control network access.

Biometric authentication

Biometric authentication relies upon a unique physical characteristic of a person to confirm his or her use of a system. Biometric identifiers include voice patterns, retinal scans, finger prints, written signatures and lip prints. When a user is to be authenticated a physical measurement must be made which is then compared against previously stored data.

Although biometric authentication is more costly than password or token based systems because of the hardware required to analyze biometric patterns, its use provides a higher level of security. For example, while someone can steal a token generating card, they cannot steal a lip or finger print, unless they first dispose of the person. Although biometric authentication provides a higher level of security than passwords and token based authentication systems its use is restricted mainly to military and very secure government applications. While the author knows of a few commercial organizations applying biometric authentication, its use is primarily as a mechanism for access to a physical area and not for direct access to stored data.

7.2 ENCRYPTION

Both hardware and software solutions to the encryption of data are readily available on the commercial marketplace. The majority of software solutions are designed to encrypt or encipher files, protecting their contents both when stored on a system as well as when transferred on a communications facility. In comparison, hardware encryption devices are primarily designed to protect data being communicated and the encryption procedure is immediately reversed at the destination of the communications path.

The most commonly used method to encrypt data is based upon Federal Information Processing Standard (FIPS) 46, which was released by the National Bureau of Standards (now the National Institute of Standards and Technology) in 1977 to provide for the cryptographic protection of federal sensitive unclassified computer information. Referred to as the Data

Encryption Standard or DES, FIPS 46 specifies the use of an algorithm which converts plaintext to ciphertext using a 56-bit key. The algorithm used to encipher data is also used with the same key to convert ciphertext back to plaintext.

The DES algorithm consists of 16 "rounds" of operations that mix data and the key together in a prescribed manner based upon a series of permutations and substitutions. The goal of the DES algorithm is to scramble the data and key completely so that every bit of the ciphertext depends upon every bit of data plus every bit of the 56-bit key.

To break an encrypted message using DES would require testing approximately 72.059 quadrillion key combinations. Using a computer capable of performing 10 million key tests per second would require approximately 228 years until the message was decrypted. Thus, in spite of a degree of controversy over the strength of the DES algorithm, it should provide sufficient strength to obscure the meaning of data until the data in the message is obsolete.

The key to the enciphering process used by DES and other cryptographic techniques is modulo 2 addition and modulo 2 subtraction. The top portion of Figure 7.1 illustrates the use of modulo 2 addition to form an enciphered bit stream, while the lower portion of that illustration shows how the original plaintext bit stream is reconstructed by using the same key but now performing a modulo 2 subtraction upon the data.

A number of vendors, including Racal–Milgs, Technical Communications Corporation and Western Datacom, market DES compatible products. In evaluating the potential use of such products you must differentiate between leased line and switched network connections.

A. Encryption	
Plaintext Data	1010
$\oplus$ Key	0111
Enciphered Data	1101
B. Decryption	
Encrypted Data	1101
$\ominus$ Key	0111
Reconstructed Plaintext Data	1010

Figure 7.1 Modulo 2 operations form the basis of enciphering and deciphering operations.

Leased line versus _switched network operations_

On a leased line transmission facility, such as a circuit connecting two remote bridges or routers, you will only require two physical encryption devices. An example of this type of network configuration is illustrated in Figure 7.2a.

If you intend to use encryptors on dial-in lines, you can consider several options. First, you can install one dial-in line, modem and datacryptor to service each remote datacryptor user, providing a one-to-one correspondence between the key used by each remote user and the key used by each datacryptor at the dial-in site. A second method you can consider is to provide two or more remote datacryptor users with the same key, having them dial either a specific telephone number or a main

a. Leased line use

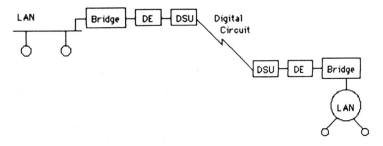

b. Switched network use

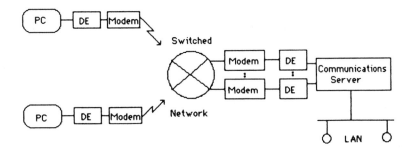

Legend DE data encrypter
DSU digital service unit

Figure 7.2 Using stand-alone data encryption devices.

rotary telephone number and contend for access to datcryptors programmed with the same key at the dial-in site.

An example of the latter is illustrated in Figure 7.2b. However, in this situation the loss of a datacryptor compromises all of the dial-in lines that use encryption devices that operate with the same key. In comparison, if each remote user had a datacryptor with a unique key to use with a specific dial-in port, the loss of a datacryptor only compromises one dial-in line. Then, if the loss is reported the network manager only has to disconnect the line serving the lost or stolen datacryptor to resolve the potential compromise.

File encryption

As an alternative to the use of hardware, you can consider software encryption products to hide the contents of a message or data you want to store or transmit to another LAN user. Some LAN E-mail application programs automatically encipher messages stored on the file server as well as when messages are transmitted between the server and a client. Other programs do not offer such protection and require the use of third party software products to hide the contents of a message from either casual observation or network monitoring. To illustrate the use of encryption, let us assume we have a message whose contents we wish to protect (see Figure 7.3).

Figure 7.4 illustrates the main menu screen generated by the program ZCrypt™ from Micanopy MicroSystems Inc. After entering "E" to encrypt, the program will prompt you to enter the filename and key to use in the encryption process. The program also supports the use of wildcards, permitting you to

---

```
TO:     Victor Kapaski
FROM:   John Smart

Thank you for your last payment. I will provide you with the
requested company information concerning future marketing plans
in outer Mongolia at precisely 5 PM on Monday. The plans will be
left in the trash container located at 212 West 48th Street. At
4:58 you should drop the package containing $12750 in small bills
in the trash container. At 5 PM I will drop my package in the con-
tainer and retrieve yours.
```

Figure 7.3 Contents of an E-mail message we wish to protect.

```
ZCrypt Version 1.2S 11/10/92 (c) 1991 Micanopy
MicroSystems, Inc.

To encrypt : ZCrypt FileName.Ext          [EncryptionMethod] [/cfm]
To decrypt : ZCrypt FileName.Ext /d       [EncryptionMethod] [/cfm]


Where EncryptionMethod can be:
 /X = High Speed (default)                /XY  ⌐
 /Y = Optimum                             /YZ  ]  Combinations. . .
 /Z = High Security                       /YZ  ⌐
                                          /XYZ = Most secure

Options:
 /CFM = Confirm each filename (when wildcard
filenames are specified)



                      F1 for Help      Escape to Quit

Edit functions:
 Enter - terminates a line                  Backspace - deletes character
                                            Ctrl-Backspace - deletes line
```

```
Encrypt or Decrypt (E/D)?
```

Figure 7.4 ZCrypt main menu.

encrypt a series of files through the use of a single command line entry.

Although ZCrypt is an excellent program for hiding the contents of a file, there are two problems associated with its use to protect an E-mail message. First, ZCrypt encrypts the entire contents of a file, which means you may have to attach the file to a conventional message for it to reach its destination. Secondly, ZCrypt is similar to almost all other encryption programs in that it does not encrypt data selectively based upon the necessity to avoid the resulting enciphered character consisting of high-ordered ASCII (8-bits) which cannot be transported by certain commercial E-mail systems.

Figure 7.5 illustrates an attempt to list the contents of the message shown in Figure 7.3 after it was encrypted using ZCrypt. Note that the resulting encrypted file can contain any of the 256 8-bit characters supported by a PC, and eventually the display of a break character terminates the display of the encrypted file prematurely. Since the contents of this file con-

```
Enter Filename: message
Confirm wildcard files? y

MESSAGE . .

B:\)type message

· §ú?\ ┼ aä ╫ ∅
  ╧ w ╙ ┘

╫ Ptīo≫ê)ü} ♩ [û╟d ÷' IÑ≈_oÜ}K: ⊦]a≡f*rHyµIøo

B: \)
```

Figure 7.5 Extended ASCII code generated by the use of ZCrypt.

tain extended ASCII characters, it cannot be transmitted via certain commercial E-mail systems that are restricted to supporting 7-bit ASCII. Thus, if your LAN was connected to a commercial E-mail system that did not support 8-bit ASCII, you would not be able to use ZCrypt as well as most other file encryption programs to hide the contents of your message and transmit the encrypted file.

As an alternative to ZCrypt and similar file encryption programs, you can consider the use of programs ENCIPHER.BAS and DECIPHER.BAS contained in the book *Top Secret: Data Encryption Techniques* By Gilbert Held, published by Howard W.S. SAMS, Indianapolis, 1994. The first program, whose initial screen display is illustrated in Figure 7.6, generates an encrypted file which does not contain any ASCII control characters or extended ASCII characters. Thus, the resulting

```
ENCIPHER.BAS enciphers text based upon the use of enciphering
techniques contained in the book:
ELECTRONIC MAIL PRIVACY: USING PRACTICAL ENCIPHERING TECHNIQUES

This program supports the use of upper and lower case letters,
digits, punctuation characters and other characters whose ASCII
values range between 32 and 128, but EXCLUDES the use of the for-
ward slash (/), backslash (\) and double quote characters.

Enter your secret code (6 characters required) : ? secret
```

Figure 7.6 Main menu of the program ENCIPHER.BAS.

encrypted file can be transmitted on commercial E-mail systems that cannot support the transmission of these characters. Another interesting feature of this program is the use of the forward slash character which disables encryption of lines prefixed with that character. This feature permits you to selectively encrypt portions of a file, where a portion of its contents should remain as plaintext to ensure it is received by the correct person.

Figure 7.7 illustrates the contents of the file CIPHERTX.DAT which contains the resulting message encrypted using the program ENCIPHER.BAS. Note that the double quotes are used by the program to represent stored strings on the file.

Use of forward slashes to prefix the originator and recipient of the message results in the bypassing of those lines from the encryption process. In addition, as observed from the listing of the encrypted file, only conventional ASCII was used to form encrypted characters which permits the contents of the file to be transmitted over commercial E-mail systems restricted to the use of 7-bit ASCII characters.

The value of file encryption can be judged by details of the FBI search of the home and CIA office of Mr Aldrich Ames, the alleged Russian spy. According to the FBI, investigators found more than 100 secret CIA cables in Mr Ames' home computer. Perhaps if Mr Ames had used an encryption program the evidence gathered by the FBI would have resembled a list of non-intelligent characters instead of the contents of CIA cables!

```
C:\>a:

A:\>type ciphertx.dat

"/TO:     Victor Kapaski"
"/FROM:   John Smart"
""
"bJIat̃  ;c}xMmln[PlKyLbsE_[KhG&xtp̂  v?1DI9[Og!X8bI3[),=i(48r1zK"
"9U.cu[fosI91#H=-sjIw-)H?HQnlh=b$4r{No U5bvey_+Ar!UyjVq,I]2CtqfU]DX"
"=$Umgl;A MI¦Z%;cJ%RL'&X!uFq8S_4c'#oDkRxecH8YIuaTd( 'Rpujs6[HOKbil;'"
"OL̂  -#c&PJTS@v#YH oFH(PeyL]IzwH_qk'apuyF$U'*F,JQh0}$S5zJ#6O, (S¦[P"
"[XJ87$}3,%% 9}¦elt$22+:M;.bgAR(WSOb@4t[qKLmdlTw:3iQK( D%ohT&¦.R"
"&wCc5¦7̂  :0q̃ B,6'5KZMYp:2 ,j!} &, $¦p_T¦E4)yx9*_j#g*,2]',YKB&2dERxî"
"}?Ẑ 'P4'Y!in=G}"
```

Figure 7.7 Ciphertex file produced by the program ENCIPHER.BAS which selectively encrypts lines in the plaintext message.

Basic encryption methods

There are three types or methods of encryption you can consider—private key encryption, public key encryption, and digital signature encryption. This section presents an overview of each method and their advantages and disadvantages.

Private key encryption

Under private key encryption a single key is shared by the originator and recipient of a message. That key must be kept secret and controlled only by the parties that have access to the key for the cryptographic process to remain secure. Otherwise, if another person has access to the key, that person can use the key to decrypt the contents of a previously encrypted message or file.

The most commonly used private key encryption is based upon the previously described Data Encryption Standard. The DES key is 56 bits long, and while its use as a private key can effectively prevent the disclosure of information, it has several limitations. First, a private key system limits the number of persons that can communicate, unless you are willing to have many persons share the same key. This widens the potential compromise of data if a person discloses his or her key or if the equipment they use to encrypt and decrypt data is lost or stolen.

Another problem associated with private key systems is the fact that they do not verify the originator of a message or document. For example, an unauthorized person could sit down at a workstation which is connected to a network by a hardware product which automatically encrypts and decrypts data flowing on the network. Although the person's message will be protected by the hardware encryption process from observation by another person using diagnostic monitoring equipment, the encryption process does not authenticate the user nor the document they created and transmitted. To do so requires a mechanism to provide or append digital signatures to documents. Such a mechanism is described later in this section.

Public key encryption

Under public key encryption, each person that has a requirement to communicate securely with other persons is provided with two keys—a public key and a private key. The two keys are mathematically related, but the private key cannot be determined from the public key.

The public key, as its name implies, can be provided to anyone and can even be fully disclosed, while the private key is kept secret and is restricted to the use of one person. A user with a message to transmit does so by encoding data using the public key of the intended recipient. Upon receipt of the message the recipient decodes it using his or her private key.

The main problem associated with the use of public keys is key management. To illustrate why key management is important, assume a person claiming to be Fred sends his public key to Tom, requesting Tom to use this public key to encrypt information when sending documents to Fred. Tom eventually uses this public key to encrypt information and sends it to the person claiming to be Fred, who can decrypt the information because his public key was used. This type of vulnerability is referred to as "spoofing" and can be prevented by the use of a digital signature.

Other problems associated with the use of public-key encryption include the processing required to encrypt and decrypt messages, and the number of keys users must know. Concerning processing power, the computations required for public key encryption require the use of more powerful computers when implemented in software, or the time to encrypt and decrypt messages will become significantly longer than with private key encryption. Concerning keys, each user must know and correctly use the public key of the intended recipient. Thus, using the wrong public key will result in the inability of the intended recipient to decrypt a message.

Digital signatures

A digital signature can be considered as a mechanism which convinces the recipient of the integrity of a message and the identity of the originator.

Digital signatures can be traced to the nuclear test ban treaty between the United States and the former Soviet Union. Under that treaty each country placed seismometers at fixed locations in the other country to monitor for the occurrence of nuclear tests. Since it was quite possible that a host country could tamper with the data from the monitoring nation's seismometers, a mechanism was required to validate that the data was indeed generated by the appropriate seismometer and was not altered. Although numerous types of authentication processes can verify the device generating the data, only digital signatures can verify both where the data came from and its integrity.

Products   Currently there are several digital signature products commercially marketed. One set of products is based upon the Digital Signature Standard (DSS) which defines a public key cryptographic system for generating and verifying digital signatures. To generate a signature on a message, the owner of the private key first applies a hash algorithm on the message. A hash algorithm is used since the complexity of digital signature algorithms would require a significant length of time to apply to a long document. Instead, a one-way hash algorithm is applied to the document to generate a short, 128-bit digital "fingerprint" which represents the document.

There are two commonly supported one-way hash algorithms in use. One hash algorithm, referred to as the Secure Hash Algorithm (SHA), is used with the Digital Signature Standard public key system developed by the National Institute of Standards and Technology (NIST). A second one-way hash algorithm known as Message Digest 5 (MD5) is used with a digital signature method developed by RSA Data Security, a commercial vendor of security products.

Under the Digital Signature Standard the owner of the private key applies the Secure Hash Algorithm to the message, resulting in the generation of a 128-bit fingerprint referred to as a message digest. The owner of the private key then applies the private key to the message digest, resulting in the generation of a digital signature. Any person who has access to the public key, message, and digital signature can then verify the signature, which in turn verifies the fact that the message was not altered. Figure 7.8 illustrates the operations involved in the generation and verification of digital signatures using DSS.

The RSA public key encryption system has been adopted by a number of vendors of software products designed to promote LAN and WAN communications security. One such product is MailSafe™, developed by Fisher International Systems Corporation of Naples, FL. Designed to operate on IBM PC and compatible computers, MailSafe is a safeguard program and does not transfer messages electronically. Instead, it permits a user to sign a file with an RSA digital signature, seal a file with an RSA

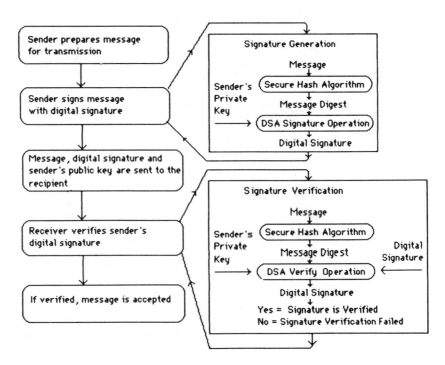

Figure 7.8 Generation and verification of digital signatures through the use of the NIST Digital Signature Standard (courtesy NIST).

digital envelope, open an RSA digital envelope with a public key and verify an RSA digital signature.

To seal a file in an RSA digital envelope, the user simply selects a file and its intended recipient through the use of a menu. Similarly, the receipt of a signed file can be easily verified through the application of the RSA digital signature by using another program menu.

MailSafe requires you to use first an accompanying program called KeyGen™. KeyGen, as its name implies, generates encryption keys, specifically public and private keys. This program requires you to enter three data items—a "login" name, your official name, and a password. The password is most critical as its duplicatability determines the security of your private MailSafe key. Thus, KeyGen requires the password to be at least 8 characters in length, as indicated in Figure 7.9, in which the attempted use of a short password generated the error message.

Once you enter a password of acceptable length, KeyGen will prompt you to press the Ctrl, Shift or Alt keys 100 times. This enables the program to use the time between key entries as ran-

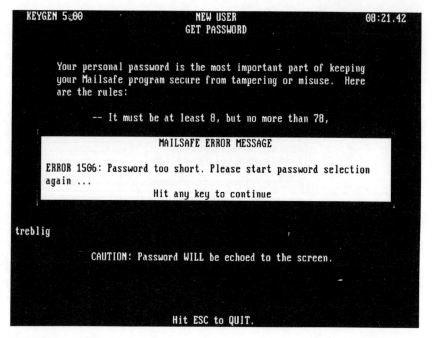

Figure 7.9 KeyGen requires a personal password between 8 and 78 characters in length.

dom input which is then used to generate your public and private keys. The public key is placed in a file with the extension .PK, while your private or secret key is placed in a file with the extension .SK. Once you have generated your public and private keys you are ready to use MailSafe.

Figure 7.10 illustrates the MailSafe main menu. Note that the program provides you with five main functions—SIGN which enables you to append your RSA Digital Signature to a file, SEAL which results in the encryption of a file by placing it in an RSA Digital Envelope, OPEN which decrypts or opens an RSA Digital Envelope sealed for you, VERIFY which provides you with the ability to verify or remove an RSA Digital Signature on a file, and UTILITIES which provides you with access to the use of a variety of utilities to include encrypting and decrypting local files, different types of file displays, public key information, and program configuration information.

The use of each MailSafe main menu option follows a similar pattern. First, you select a file to operate the option upon. Mail-Safe provides you with an easy-to-use file selection capability as indicated by Figure 7.11, in which the files in the default RSA

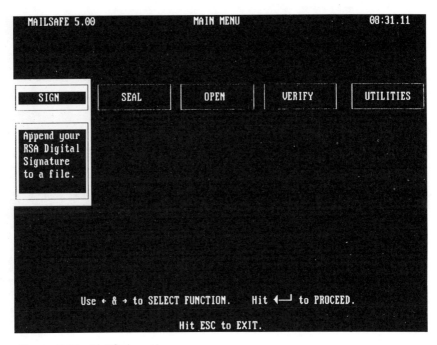

Figure 7.10 MailSafe main menu.

directory are listed and the author decided he wanted to select the directory PCPLUS. On typing simply C:\PCPLUS the program generates the box superimposed in the middle of Figure 7.11, and pressing the Enter key changes the directory to the newly entered directory. For each selected directory the program displays a highlight bar which you can move over a filename to complete the selection of a file within a specified directory. Once a file is selected you can perform an operation on the file based upon the main menu option you are using. For example, if you previously selected the SIGN option, once you select a file the program will allow you to sign the file.

Since a picture is worth a thousand words, let us follow a short series of screen images which illustrate the addition of an RSA Digital Signature to a file. Figure 7.12 illustrates the resulting contents of the directory PCPLUS on drive C based upon the entry of that directory in Figure 7.11. Note that the highlight bar is placed over the file NW, which is the file to which we will add a digital signature.

Once you select a file and press the Enter key, MailSafe will display summary information about the file. This is indicated in Figure 7.13 which illustrates the resulting display generated

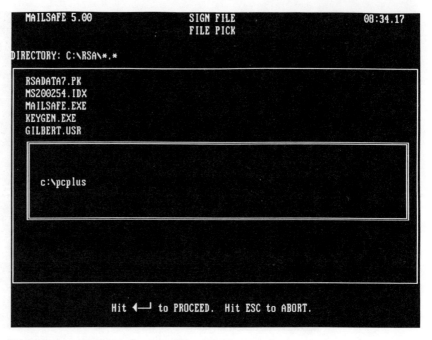

```
MAILSAFE 5.00              SIGN FILE              08:34.17
                           FILE PICK

DIRECTORY: C:\RSA\*.*

    RSADATA7.PK
    MS200254.IDX
    MAILSAFE.EXE
    KEYGEN.EXE
    GILBERT.USR

    ┌─────────────────────────────────────────────────┐
    │                                                   │
    │   c:\pcplus                                       │
    │                                                   │
    │                                                   │
    └─────────────────────────────────────────────────┘




          Hit ◄──┘ to PROCEED.  Hit ESC to ABORT.
```

Figure 7.11   Changing to the PCPLUS directory.

by MailSafe after you select a file, assuming you first selected the SIGN option from the program's main menu. From this summary file information screen you can press Enter to sign the file, the Space bar to display the contents of the file, or Escape to return to the file selection screen.

Let us now assume you press the Enter key to sign the file with your RSA Digital Signature. If you then press the Space bar and scroll through the file you can view the resulting signature appended to the end of the file. Figure 7.14 illustrates the RSA Digital Signature added to the previously selected file named NW. Note that the program automatically changes the filename to NW.SIG as indicated in the upper left portion of Figure 7.14.

Most MailSafe operations are intuitive and the program can be used to both encrypt the contents of a file and to verify the originator of a file.

LAN considerations

In general there are two methods you can consider to protect the flow of information on a LAN—selective and inclusive

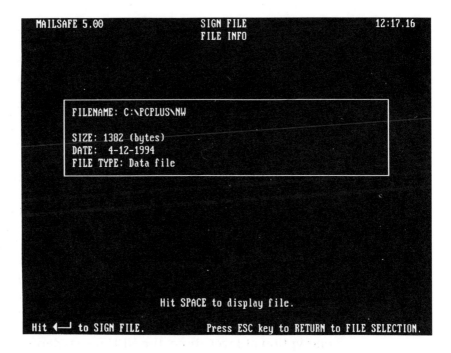

```
MAILSAFE 5.00              SIGN FILE                  12:16.17
                           FILE PICK

DIRECTORY: C:\PCPLUS\*.*
                                                       MORE →
   PCINSTAL.EXE  GIF-FORM.AT-  PCPLUS.USR    DOWJONES.ASP  GIFEXE41.ZIP
   PCPLUS.EXE    DELTAC.TAR    PCBOARD.ASP   GRCP2.ARC     TATGET.ASP
   LZ.SIG        LJVGAPNT.ZIP  ALEC          PORTS.ASP     XEMOTE.ASP
   PCEDIT.EXE    QUADTREE.TAR  FLOAT.RTE     RBBS.ASP      MCI.ASP
   PCKEYMAP.EXE  XARC.EXE      CMPRSN.DOC    REMOTE.ASP    PCPLUS.KBD
   DSTORM.ASP    INSTALL.EXE   KERMIT.RTE    HUFF1.EXE     DIALS.ASP
   PCMAIL.EXE    PCPLUS.HHP    NEOPNT.ZIP    CVTGIF.ARC    ULTRA3D.EXE
   PCSETUP.EXE   YYY           HOOK.SIG      DECODER.C     PCPLUS.KEY
   THEYHERE.ARC  PCPLUS.ICO    MODEMS.DAT    ESCTIME.DTP   PCPLUS.PRM
   PCHELP.RTE    JFIF.EXE      NW░░░░░░░░    HOSTKEYS.DTP  XXX
   PCPLUS.FON    TCPAKA.EXE    XARCPLUS.EXE  PADCHAR.DTP   PORTS.ASX
   PCPLUS.HLP    ULTRA3D.ZIP   GRAFCT31.ZIP  DISKOUNT.ZIP  PCPLUS.XLT
   PRNTGF.ZIP    PCPLUS.PIF    PW            JPL9401.ZIP   ERRS.H
   JJSB0393.ZIP  ASPCOMP.EXE   ULTRA3D.DOC   CJPEG.EXE     Q.EXE
   PCPLUS.SCR    CONVERT.EXE   BJACK.ASP     PCPLUS.DIR    HUFFST.ZIP
   COMPR.TXT     DIET143.ZIP   CSERVE.ASP    HOST.ASP      LIST90E.EXE

              · Use Home ↑ PgUp → ← End ↓ PgDn keys to SELECT FILE,
          or TYPE IN desired filename or directory (? and * are allowed).
               Hit ←— to PROCEED.  Hit ESC key to RETURN to MAIN MENU.
```

Figure 7.12   Using MailSafe to select a file in the directory PCPLUS.

```
MAILSAFE 5.00              SIGN FILE                  12:17.16
                           FILE INFO




        FILENAME: C:\PCPLUS\NW

        SIZE: 1382 (bytes)
        DATE:  4-12-1994
        FILE TYPE: Data file







                  Hit SPACE to display file.

   Hit ←— to SIGN FILE.          Press ESC key to RETURN to FILE SELECTION.
```

Figure 7.13   Summary file information displayed by MailSafe.

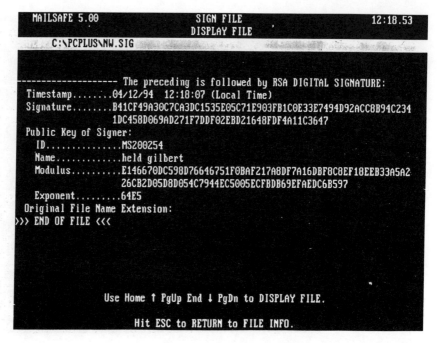

Figure 7.14 Viewing the RSA Digital Signature added to the previously selected file.

encryption. Selective encryption occurs through the use of file encryption software or the use of a LAN application program which automatically encrypts the contents of E-mail messages stored on a server or in transit between a client workstation and server.

To obtain inclusive encryption requires the use of a special type of encryption device which must be able to recognize the format of LAN frames and only encrypt information carried in the information field of each frame. Otherwise, the encryption of destination addresses would not permit the bridging or routing of data from one network to another.

One example of an inclusive encryption product is the series of Network Encryption Units (NEUs) manufactured by Semaphore Communications Corporation of Santa Clara, CA. That firm's NEUs support LAN packet encryption at layer two (the data link layer) or layer three (the network layer). When encrypting at layer two, the NEU encrypts all data past the layer two header. Non-routable protocols, such as DecNet LAT, which are not intended to leave the LAN, are encrypted at layer two. For encryption at layer three, the NEU must identify different protocols since the information field location differs based upon the protocol. Protocols that can be encrypted by the Semaphore NEU include IP, XNS, IPX, DecNet Phase IV, Banyan IP, and Appletalk. Since the layer three header is not encrypted this permits the packet to be routed.

Figure 7.15 illustrates the use of Semaphore NEUs to protect traffic flowing on an Ethernet as well as between an Ethernet and Token-Ring network. At the time this book was written, Semaphore did not market an NEU that could be used to support individual workstations on a Token-Ring network. Thus, while intra-Ethernet and inter-LAN communications are protected, the NEUs could not provide intra-Token-Ring communications protection.

Applications

If your communications security requirement is limited to protecting certain applications, such as E-mail, you can consider using encryption as an evaluation factor in your procurement action. Doing so may alleviate the necessity of obtaining special-

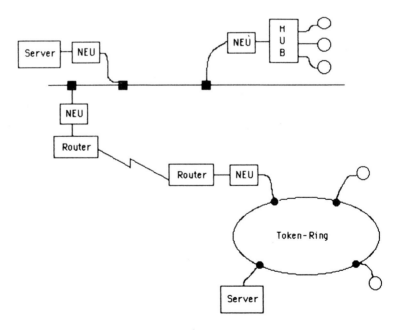

Figure 7.15 Using Semaphore network encryption units.

ized hardware as well as the cost associated with such hardware.

For example, Lotus Developments, cc:Mail automatically encrypts passwords, messages and all mail attachments. In addition, cc:Mail also stores its messages in encrypted form in its database post office repository. Thus, the use of cc:Mail also eliminates the necessity of acquiring a stand-alone utility to encrypt your organization's message center repository.

Other LAN electronic mail programs that provide different levels of encryption include Beyond Mail from Beyond Inc. of Cambridge, MA, and Microsoft Mail from Microsoft Corporation of Redmond, WA, among others.

7.3 SECURITY MODEMS

Security modems are relatively old communications products that were first developed during the 1970s to add protection for dial-in access to mainframes and minicomputers. The earliest category of security modems were normally limited to an authorization code/callback operation. That is, a user accessing the modem from a remote location would enter an authorization code which the modem would compare with a table of predefined codes entered by the network administrator. Assuming the modem matched the authorization code with an entry in its table, it would disconnect the user, retrieve a telephone number associated with the authorization code and originate a call to that number. The user would place their modem in its answer mode of operation to receive the returned call. Once the new connection was established the remote user would then proceed to attempt to gain access to the desired computational facility by entering their user ID.

Call-back operations

The call-back operation of a security modem prevents unauthorized access by location checking to a network, since it only permits an attempt to access network resources from predefined telephone numbers. In a LAN environment the use of a security modem with a call-back capability should be considered for use if employees are provided a LAN dial-in capability to check E-mail and perform other activities. Obviously, the call-back feature is primarily applicable for access from fixed locations, as it would be an administrative nightmare to constantly program the telephone numbers of traveling salespersons.

Encryption and authentication tokens

In addition to a call-back feature, some security modem vendors added encryption and authentication tokens to their products. As we saw earlier in this chapter, encryption scrambles data into an unintelligible form for transmission over telephone lines, which protects the content of information from interception. The use of an authentication tokens verifies the identity of the user at the remote site. Encryption was previously described in this chapter, while the use of tokens was discussed in Chapter 2.

If your primary goal is to ensure employees can access LAN facilities from their homes without exposing your network to hackers, the use of call-back security modems may suffice. If you also require security from potential monitoring of communications lines, you must then consider a built-in or stand-alone encryption capability. However, encryption requires an effective key management procedure which adds an additional administrative burden.

The use of a constantly changing access token displayed by credit card sized token generators adds an additional degree of security from unauthorized eavesdroppers who may overlook the entry of a token. Since the token typically changes every 60 seconds, the number observed will be invalid when the unauthorized user attempts to access a token based system.

Token based access to security modems requires LAN compliant software which normally operates on a separate network security server. The security modems will include built-in ROM code which enables communications between the security modem and the security server. Normally, security modems will be connected to the network via a communications server, so actual communications between the modem and the token verification software occur between servers.

Figure 7.16 illustrates the use of Telebit Corporation (Sunnyvale, CA) security modems with token security software marketed by Security Dynamics Corporation (Chelmsford, MA). Telebit modems connect to the vendor's NetBlazer router which supports TCP/IP, Apple ARA and Novell IPX based networks. The Security Dynamics ACE/Server transfers updated tokens to

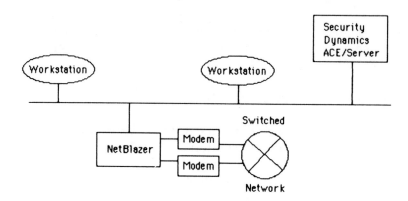

Figure 7.16   Telebit NetBlazer with SecurID token validation support.

each Telebit modem, permitting the modem to verify the token entered by the remote user. Since the user-entered token is designed to serve as verification of a person's identity, it can be used in place of callbacks. In addition, it provides a significant degree of flexibility for use by persons who must access a LAN from different locations. For example, an executive traveling to five cities could easily access a LAN through its dial-in security token checking modem. In comparison, it would be difficult or impossible to have the callback feature of security modems connect the executive through the PBXs typically used by hotels.

8

ADMINISTRATIVE SECURITY

Administrative security is the policies, procedures and application of technology to protect data resources. Since the actual composition and location of data resources as well as the structure of the building where they are located and background of employees differs between organizations, we can also reasonably expect administrative security measures to differ. This means it is highly doubtful that two organizations will employ the same set of administrative security policies and procedures, it does not mean an organization can forego implementing administrative security policies and procedures.

Administrative security can be considered as the glue which bonds together all elements associated with the protection of LAN resources, and provides for the orderly restoral of operations if a disaster should strike.

The key to the implementation of appropriate policies and procedures is what this author refers to as a "network bible". This document supplements the implementation of policies and procedures required to protect LAN resources but does not include policies and procedures as they are normally maintained in an administrative manual.

Due to the importance of the network bible for implementing effective administrative security policies and procedures we will first focus our attention upon this important document. Once we obtain an appreciation for the contents and placement of this extremely important document we will turn our attention to the different categories of administrative policies and procedures you can consider. In doing so we will examine a core set of policies and procedures you can consider when developing administrative security guidelines to meet the specific requirements of your organization.

8.1 THE NETWORK BIBLE

The network bible is a special type of document which must be periodically updated to reflect changes in your network. As such, it can be considered to represent a "living document" which will be maintained as long as you have your network.

Contents

To obtain an appreciation for the contents of a network bible requires an understanding of the goal behind the creation of this document. That goal is to enable network facilities to be reconstructed in a minimum amount of time regardless of the type of disaster that may strike. The network bible will document both your network and your human resources. Concerning the latter, entries in the network bible can range in scope from the listing of key personnel to detailed information about each network user.

Although the specific contents of a network bible will vary, we can obtain an appreciation of the key items for inclusion by examining the major components of a typical LAN. This will provide us with the opportunity to relate specific hardware and software inventory and configuration data to their inclusion in the network bible.

Workstations

Table 8.1 lists workstation information you should consider for inclusion in a network bible. In addition to providing the information necessary to reconstruct the operation of a workstation in the event of a network disaster, the recording of information listed in Table 8.1 will facilitate recovery of workstation operations from a localized workstation disaster, such as the failure of a hard drive or the operation of a virus which destroys critical hard disk information.

Note that many of these entries are far more than a one-line entry in a book. Some entries, such as key file configurations, may be represented in the network bible as a listing or as the filename on an accompanying diskette. Concerning the latter, the policy of the organization may be such that one person is

Table 8.1 Network bible workstation information.

Workstation location	Software
Authorized user	Operating system
Hardware configuration	Key file configuration(s)
Computer	AUTOEXEC.BAT
CMOS configuration	CONFIG.SYS
Memory	Application programs used
BIOS	Locally resident
Vendor	Network resident
Revision	Backup
Diskette drive(s)	Last performed
Hard disk	Tape number
Capacity	Network information
Partition(s)	Connection to hub
Adapter card(s)	Port assignment
Type	Cabling
Vendor(s)	Login script
Revision level	

assigned to periodically copy key configuration files to disk using a predefined naming convention scheme which facilitates the identification of those files to specific workstations. The naming convention scheme is a most important consideration, since most workstations will use the same file name for a core set of key files which govern the operation of the workstation.

While it can be argued that a disaster which adversely effects the use of the building where equipment currently operates would probably result in the acquisition of new hardware that may not duplicate existing equipment, the appropriate recording of workstation information will significantly assist making a workstation operational in a minimal amount of time. In addition, the recording of information listed in Table 8.1 can provide significant assistance in maintaining the operational status of equipment. For example, consider the failure of the battery of a PC whose operation is vital for maintaining the CMOS memory configuration of the computer which is important for the operating system to identify and effectively use the hard disk. When the battery fails, CMOS stored data is erased, preventing the computer from being successfully initialized. Without access to the network bible or a similar document which lists the CMOS configuration, a five-minute battery replacement and CMOS configuration effort can easily turn into several hours or more of work when the computer user attempts to enter a new sequence of CMOS configuration data elements.

It is important to note that the information in the network bible is designed principally to facilitate the recovery of equipment adversely affected by different types of threats. As such, the network bible will directly include listings of key configuration files, but for more extensive information the document will serve as a reference to the location of backup information for each workstation. Thus, the person responsible for maintaining the network bible might periodically copy a user's backup tape, label the tape, and store it at an appropriate location where it could be retrieved in the event of a major building problem. Now that we have an indication of the type of workstation information that should be included in a network bible let's turn our attention to the type of server information that should be placed in that document.

File server

You should consider recording a core set of information for each network file server. That information is listed in Table 8.2.

Table 8.2 Network bible file server information.

Server location	Software
Authorized user(s)	LAN operating system
Hardware configuration	Site license information
Computer type	Operating system configuration
CMOS configuration	Directory structure
Memory	Permissions
BIOS	Key file configurations
Vendor	Startup
Revision	Login script(s)
Diskette drive(s)	Application programs
Hard disk	Description
Capacity	Site license information
Partition(s)	User information
Adapter card(s)	Backup information
Type	Last performed or schedule
Vendor(s)	Tape number assignment
Revision level	Network information
Disk array	Connection to hub
	Port assignment(s)
	Cabling

Note that many entries are very similar to those elements you will want to record for individual workstations, especially information concerning the hardware platform. Concerning the hardware platform, the entries in both Tables 8.1 and 8.2 are oriented towards the use of PC type computers. You can alter the recorded information elements to reflect the type of computer system used as a platform for a workstation or file server, however, those elements listed in the referenced tables provide a reasonable level of detail you can modify to reflect the use of other types of computer systems.

For both the LAN operating system as well as applications running on file servers, it is a good idea to record specific site license information. In the event of a building disaster or destruction of the file server upon which the software operated, you may require such information to enable the legitimate use of those programs on a new hardware platform.

The backup information can simply reference a numbering scheme used to create and label backup tapes as well as their location.

Human resources

Recovery of an individual workstation or an entire network is dependent upon the efforts of organizational employees and may be dependent upon the efforts of vendor personnel. Thus, no network bible will be complete without including a significant amount of human resources information.

Table 8.3 indicates human resources data elements you may wish to consider incorporating into a network bible. In examining the entries in Table 8.3 readers should note that actual human resources information incorporated into your network bible will be based upon the size of your network, your geo-

Table 8.3 Network bible human resources information.

Key employee directory 　Name 　Address 　Telephone number 　Alternative points of contact 　Field(s) of specialization 　Special training	Departmental directory 　Points of contact Vendor directory 　Technical support 　Sales support

graphic location and other factors that can effect your requirement for certain types of information. For example, a 20-station LAN located in a small town where everyone knows everybody would probable require less detailed human resource information than a 250-station LAN located in a major city where most employees have little knowledge of the person behind the next partition.

In recording human resources information, the basic rule to follow is to include enough information to identify who to contact and how they can be contacted. It is important to note that the network bible is not a substitute for administrative procedures. Thus, it is not normally used as the document to indicate when employees should be called in the event of an emergency, since that information is typically included in an organization's policies and procedures document.

One of the key sets of information often overlooked in constructing a network bible concerns vendor contacts. While such information as well as almost all other information in the network bible can eventually be reconstructed, in an emergency you may not have the luxury of time. In addition, there is no assurance that the creator of the network bible will survive a disaster. Thus, vendor information should include as much point-of-contact information as possible should be included to facilitate recovery operations by any organizational employee tasked with using the network bible to restore all or a portion of a failed network.

Inter-LAN data elements

An important and often overlooked set of data elements that belong in a network bible concern the connection of your LAN to other networks, a topic we refer to as inter-LAN data elements. These can include bridge, router and gateway hardware and software configurations, information concerning communications carrier facilities used to interconnect LANs via wide area network (WAN) communications facilities, WAN communications equipment configurations, and vendor technical and sales contact information.

Updating

The key to the effective use of a network bible is to ensure it contains the information required to facilitate the restoral of network operations. This means the document must be updated periodically to reflect changes in your network, the acquisition of new hardware and software, employee turnover, and similar events that can effect the restoral of network operations.

Owing to the dynamic nature of LANs, it is entirely conceivable that one or more data elements can change on a daily basis. However, from a practical point of view you will want to balance the effort involved in updating a network bible against its aged value. In doing so you will attempt to select a reasonable update frequency which will permit the document to serve its useful purpose if an occasion arises without becoming an administrative burden throughout the year. For most organizations a quarterly or semi-annual update will provide an acceptable network bible which will form the basis for recovery and restoral operations.

Placement

For the same reason you would not leave the combination to a safe posted on its door, you should not leave the only copy of your network bible in your office. Since disaster knows no boundaries, it is a good procedure to have multiple copies of your network bible, distributing one or more copies to an off-site location.

If your organization operates legacy mainframes you probably use an off-site tape storage location. On a periodic basis copies of your organization's disk saves are transported to that site for storage, while aged previously saved backups are returned to your mainframe data center. Then it is usually a relatively easy process to add the movement and storage of a network bible to the tape cycle.

If your organization does not have a legacy mainframe, you might consider rotating updated copies of your network bible to an off-site storage location used to provide offsite LAN data storage. In Chapter 9 we will discuss the use of off-site data storage and rotation methods you can consider to maintain copies of LAN files.

8.2 ADMINISTRATIVE POLICIES AND PROCEDURES

In this section we turn our attention to administrative policies and procedures you can consider to protect your LAN resources.

As previously discussed, administrative policies and procedures are normally completely separate from the network bible. Although they may closely reference the use of information in the network bible, each document typically originates from a different organizational entity and serves to govern entirely different functions.

A policies and procedures document details how users obtain access to a network, their ability to download information from bulletin board systems onto the network, the frequency with which passwords are changed, the mechanism by which a disaster is declared and who is initially called, and similar information. In comparison, the network bible contains information required to recover from a disaster, as it documents how computers are used, contains key file listings, indicates personnel and vendor contacts, lists the location of backup tapes, and provides similar information required to facilitate the restoration of a single workstation or all of the workstations and servers on a network.

Once administrative policies and procedures are developed their frequency of change is significantly less than for the network bible. Thus, policies and procedures come in a more stable document which governs network facilities, while the network bible changes to reflect changes in the network and network users. Concerning the originators of those documents, the policies and procedures document is normally prepared by administrative personnel in conjunction with members of the networking staff. In comparison, the network bible is normally prepared exclusively by the networking staff.

Now that we have a general feeling for the differences between these two important documents, we will examine some of the policies you may wish to consider to govern the protection of LAN resources. Readers should note that the policies and procedures discussed in the remainder of this chapter are listed as guidelines and are not fixed in concrete. In fact, those policies and procedures will differ considerably between organizations due to differences in the use of networks, different types of potential threats to LAN resources and different organizational requirements for the operation and utilization of network resources.

To assist readers responsible for developing policies and procedures the remainder of this chapter contains a series of tables which indicate, by the use of questions, policies and procedures you may wish to consider when developing an appropriate manual concerning the operation and utilization of organizational computing equipment.

General policies

Table 8.4 lists a series of questions to consider prior to developing general policies that effect the operation of your LAN. The answers to some of these questions will perhaps raise an awareness that other questions must also be answered to obtain an effective set of policies and procedures.

For example, consider the question concerning the instal-

Table 8.4 General policy questions.

1	How are potential hazards to the network identified and reported? Who is responsible for their review?
2	What is the policy concerning the acquisition of hardware and software?
3	Is there an acceptable list of products departmental employees can purchase directly? If so, how are products added to that list?
4	How are suspicious incidents and potential or actual security breaches reported? What is the procedure for checking those reports?
5	How are network outages reviewed?
6	How do you perform security testing?
7	What is the policy concerning providing a security briefing for personnel? At what frequency are refresher briefings performed?
8	What is the policy concerning the use of employee electrical equipment in their work areas?
9	What is the policy concerning the use of coffee machines, heaters and other personal electrical devices located in employee work areas or other building locations?
10	What is the policy concerning the evacuation of the building when an alarm sounds?
11	What is the policy concerning the installation and checking of fire and water sensors? Where are they located?
12	Who issues badges, keys, cipher lock codes? What is the procedure for their issuance? What is the procedure for their turn-in or change when an employee leaves the organization?
13	Who is responsible for preparing and maintaining the disaster recovery plan?
14	How often is the disaster recovery plan tested? Is testing disruptive or non-disruptive?
15	Does the disaster recovery plan include the use of a hot or cold site? If so, how is the use of the site coordinated?

lation and checking of fire and water sensors. In the event of a fire, employees should be instructed to turn off all electrical equipment prior to leaving the building. Otherwise, the fans included in most computers might suck in soot caused by a small fire and turn a minor amount of damage into a major data recovery operation.

Access control

Table 8.5 lists a series of questions whose answers can be beneficial in developing appropriate access control policies and procedures. While the primary purpose of access control is to prevent the unauthorized use of network resources, this area also involves the procedures to add additional workstations to a network and provide users of those workstations with the ability to access network facilities.

You will more than likely expand upon the answers to the

Table 8.5 Access control questions.

1	What physical access controls are required to govern the use of computer equipment?
2	Where are workstations and servers located?
3	Who has permission to use and control the operation of servers? How is that permission granted?
4	What is the policy concerning the operational state of equipment when a person leaves their work area?
5	What is the policy concerning the use of passwords to gain access to each desktop computer?
6	Who is responsible for issuing and changing network passwords?
7	What is the frequency by which network passwords are changed?
8	How does a user obtain authorization to use the network and obtain a password?
9	Is there a requirement for additional security beyond the use of conventional passwords? If so, should tokens, authentication signatures or other techniques be used and how should they be used?
10	What procedures should be followed to add a workstation to the network?
11	What procedures govern the removal of obsolete user ID information when a person leaves the organization?
12	What is the policy governing the use of intruder detection and lockout features built into many network operating systems?

questions contained in Table 8.5 to ask the traditional newspaper reporter's series of questions for many subjects. For
example, concerning passwords, who issues them, when are
they issued, how are they issued, and in what form are they
issued?

Communications control

Communications control governs both intra-LAN and inter-LAN
transfer of data. Concerning intra-LAN communications, unless
special types of data encryption devices are used by workstations the contents of the information field of each frame can be
viewed by the use of diagnostic test equipment. Thus, control
of the use of such equipment is an important consideration that
is overlooked by many organizations.

To protect inter-LAN communications you can program
bridges and routers to pass data originating only from predefined source addresses, a technique commonly referred to as
"building a firewall". Another method of communications control involves the policies and procedures that govern dial access
into and out of the LAN. Table 8.6 lists a series of appropriate
questions whose answers you should consider in developing
communications control policies and procedures.

Table 8.6 Communications control questions.

1	What is the policy concerning the use of modems to obtain dial-in/dial-out capability from individual workstations?
2	Should a modem pool be permitted? If so, what restrictions, if any, govern its use?
3	Is encryption required to protect remote access to the LAN? If so, what type of encryption key (public or private) is used, who maintains the master key list, who is responsible for implementing key changes, and at what frequency do those changes occur?
4	Should callback/security modems be used? If so, what features should the modems have and what is the policy concerning the use of that type of modem?
5	Who has access to diagnostic test equipment and what is the policy concerning its use?
6	Are firewalls to be created through programming bridges and routers to permit data only from certain source addresses? If so, who determines the addresses, who is responsible for their encoding and maintenance?

Data control and recovery

The control of data involves many facets, including its editing, validation and protection. Thus, the questions contained in Table 8.7 involve the development of policies and procedures that affect the validity of data as well as its protection from unauthorized access. In addition to controlling access to data, you must consider actions that facilitate its recovery in the event of an equipment failure, fire, flood or humidity problem. By considering actions to take in the event of different types of problems, you will position your organization to obtain a faster recovery state than organizations that only consider those questions after a problem arises.

One of the questions involves the use of a uniform data recovery product. This not only simplifies procurement and operational issues but can also facilitate recovery operations. For example, one diagnostic test and recovery program automatically creates and updates an image of the hard disk partition area each time a workstation is powered on. By creating a network script file to copy the workstation image file to the network server, you can use the network to backup the vital data of the workstation if the recovery of the workstation is required due to a disk crash, virus, or another problem. Thus, the use of third party software products along with the software tools built into

Table 8.7 Data control and recovery questions.

1	What edit and validation controls are required for the construction of critical data elements in key databases?
2	What is the policy concerning the use of downloaded software or programs brought from home?
3	Should workstations and file servers be protected by the use of virus scanning and filtering software?
4	Who assigns network rights and permissions, how are they assigned, and when and why can they be changed?
5	When is the use of file encryption software authorized?
6	What is the policy and procedure when a hard drive is damaged?
7	Should a uniform type of data recovery product be used? If so, what brand, how is it used, and who uses it to recover files?
8	What is the policy concerning the removal of data from the building?
9	How is the integrity of stored data verified after a fire, flood or a problem with humidity control?

many network operating systems provides a significant capability to use the network to backup individual workstations.

Software control

The operation of new applications on a network can result in a series of problems, several of which can adversely affect the integrity of data. This is especially true when organizations fail to distinguish between test and production files when implementing new applications.

Another area of concern with respect to software control involves the testing of new applications and the implementation and verification of network operating system security controls. In addition to determining that new applications are compatible with existing applications on the network, you should ensure new applications do not introduce trap doors that permit an end run around existing security methods. One method to do this is through the application of appropriate network operating system security controls to each application added to the network, by having policies and procedures in effect to do so. Table 8.8 lists a number of appropriate questions concerning software control whose answers will provide a valuable insight for developing appropriate policies and procedures.

Backup control

Table 8.9 lists five key questions to assist you in developing policies and procedures concerning the backup of network data.

Table 8.8 Software control questions.

1	Is an audit trail required for certain software products? If so, who reviews the audit trail, what is the frequency of review?
2	Should new LAN applications be tested for compatibility with the network and other applications? If so, when are the tests conducted, who performs the tests and what criteria is used to analyze the test results?
3	What is the policy governing the use of network operating system security controls?
4	Who verifies the use of network operating system security controls? What is the frequency of verification?
5	What distinction is made between test files and production files? How are production files excluded from testing?

Table 8.9 Backup control questions.

1	What type of backups are performed (incremental or full), what equipment is backed up and when are backups performed?
2	What tape numbering scheme is used to identify backups?
3	When and how are backups moved off-site? Where are they located? Who has access to the backup site?
4	How often are backup tapes tested? Do tests occur on random tape pulls, full saves or incremental saves?
5	What procedure is followed if the backup fails?

Note that a portion of the first question concerns determining what equipment is backed up. As previously noted in this chapter, you can use script files to automate the backup of workstation data to file servers. You can also consider the use of script or batch files to automate the transfer of file server data to other file servers if they are located in different geographical areas and your organization has the transmission bandwidth between networks to permit appropriate file transfers in a reasonable amount of time. Doing so provides you with another option that can supplement conventional tape backup.

Concerning the movement of tapes to off-site storage locations, it is important to test those tapes periodically. In one situation that the author is intimately aware of, a defective tape drive was used for a long time to generate unreadable tapes. Luckily for the organization, a decision to retrieve a previously stored set of tapes uncovered the problem prior to a disaster resulting in the knowledge that recovery was not possible!

CONTINGENCY PLANNING

In Chapter 8 we discussed a variety of elements you should consider for inclusion in a network bible and administrative policies and procedures governing the operation and utilization of network resources. The goal of every organization is to prevent a disaster, but some acts of God as well as human oversights can eventually result in problems that adversely affect the organization's computational resources. When this occurs, an effective contingency plan will enable the organization to regain the use of its data in a timely and effective manner.

Due to the importance of contingency planning we conclude this book by focusing on several key aspects of this important area which allows us to anticipate a variety of potential problems as well as actions to take to resolve those problems. Contingency planning differs from conventional planning in that the former normally commences with a large number of assumptions while normal planning efforts are based upon facts and a limited number of assumptions. For example, your organization's contingency plan may include sections based upon assumptions such as that your building is hit by a tornado and totally destroyed, or a fire breaks out and renders the building unusable for several weeks, or the communications carrier serving your building has a flood in their central office which interrupts communications to your building for a week. Each assumption would then set the parameters to be overcome for the contingency planning process.

The ultimate goal of contingency planning is to develop procedures which result in the availability of information and the resources to use such information when a disaster occurs.

There are numerous types of disasters when viewed from a network user's perspective. If we define a disaster as the inability to use the computational resources within a building where we work, this definition provides the rationale for considering the use of hot and cold sites as well as an off-site data storage facility, all key elements of an effective contingency plan. Thus, the focus of this chapter is upon those three topics since their inclusion in a disaster recovery plan also provides for the ability to recover from minor disasters, such as the failure of an individual computer or file server, or the unexpected arrival of a virus which wipes out the contents of one or more hard drives.

9.1 OFF-SITE DATA STORAGE

There are several methods you can consider for moving data to an off-site storage location, as well as the operation of the site. This section will examine the options you can consider for both the movement of data as well as the operation of the off- site data storage site.

The conventional approach to the transfer of data to an off-site storage location is based upon the requirements of mainframe computer users and the time required to create backup tapes of large amounts of data stored on disk.

Full and incremental saves

Owing to the amount of data stored on disk, most mainframe sites use two types of backup—full saves and incremental saves. Depending upon the operational requirements of the mainframe site, full saves are normally performed once a week, typically sometime after midnight on Saturday. In comparison, incremental saves which represent changes to data occurring since the last full save are run every evening.

In the event of a disaster the use of the full save and an appropriate number of daily incremental saves provides the data necessary to restore the database to its condition on the evening prior to the disaster.

For transaction processing environments, such as reservation systems where tens of thousands of transactions can occur each day, the use of full and incremental saves does not provide a sufficient level of backup for protecting organizational data. These organizations, as well as others require a more current mechanism for the backup of data, typically use a technique commonly referred to as "televaulting".

Televaulting

Televaulting can be considered as the automatic read or near-read time transfer of data center files to an off-site location. To accomplish this type of data transfer requires the use of a communications facility between the host site and the backup data storage site, as well as special software which recognizes changes to previously stored data and either transfers those changes or an entire record in which a data field was changed. At the backup site, software updates the backed-up data so that the backup site has a near mirror image of the primary site.

LAN televaulting

Several vendors now offer software products which can be used to televault data stored on a LAN. Many mainframe sites tele-vault information on a real-time or near real-time basis, but most LAN televaulting products batch transactions and use the switched telephone network to transfer information periodically.

Figure 9.1 illustrates the televaulting of LAN file server information to another site. That site can be another company location or the location of a vendor that provides off-site data storage and/or a hot or cold site facility. Software operating on the file server performs the televaulting operation by batching updates and periodically dialing an off-site backup location.

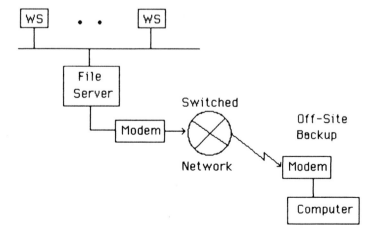

Figure 9.1 Televaulting LAN data.

Once a connection is established, the batched changes are transferred to a computer at the off-site location that has a large-capacity disk or is connected to a disk array. Periodically, usually on weekends, the off-site computer runs a program which changes the incremental transactions into a fully backed-up version of LAN file server storage.

Operational and economic considerations

Although the televaulting operation can provide a mirror image of the contents of your file servers, there are several operational and economic considerations that may make this technique unsuitable for some organizations.

From an operational perspective, televaulting file server data by itself may not be sufficient, since many employees maintain important files on their workstations. Thus, you may wish to consider the periodic transfer of workstation files to the file server for transfer to the off-site location. To automate this process, you can create a login script which automatically copies key workstation files to the file server each time a user logs into the network or at certain times on certain days. As an alternative, you can obtain a third party product which will "televault" file updates to the file server, from which those updates will be batched for televaulting to the off-site location.

Since the transfer of information to the off-site location can include proprietary data, televaulting may result in a security risk. To alleviate this risk some televaulting products automatically encrypt data prior to its transfer. Other products also perform compression on batched data to reduce the duration and cost of communications.

From an economic perspective, televaulting requires the use of a separate computer system and large-capacity hard disk or disk array at the off-site location. In comparison, conventional tape transfer does not require a dedicated computer system. Other economic factors that must be considered include the cost of televaulting software, communications hardware and the use of the switched network. Depending upon the storage capacity of your network file servers and their frequency of update, the annual cost for televaulting can easily exceed $50 000 during the first year of operation. Depending upon the frequency of data storage updates, it may be more economical to use a leased line to connect the LAN to the off-site location.

Software product functionality

When considering televaulting it is important to distinguish between software products that supplement full tape backups and other products that have the capability to convert a series of batched transactions into a mirror image of a file server's storage. The first type of product simply transports batched changes via a communications facility to a distant location for storage. You must then use another software product to update the last full save with the stored batched changes in the event of a disaster which requires data recovery.

A second type of televaulting product can use full save tapes but does not depend upon their use. This type of televaulting product in effect has the ability to convert periodic batched transactions, which you can consider to represent a series of incremental saves, into a full save.

9.2 HOT AND COLD SITES

A *hot* site is a location which contains operational computer equipment, whose use you contract for in the event of an emergency. Hot sites were developed originally to provide a facility where organizations could send their data files, application programs, and personnel to reconstruct their operations if their own data center became unusable. The first hot site was established in the early 1980s and the success of the concept resulted in over 80 companies marketing hot sites by the mid 1990s.

Since local area networks postdated the development of hot sites, it was not until the early 1990s that hot site locations began to recognize the importance of client-server computing to organizations that were previously dependent upon centralized mainframe data centers. Since then, many hot sites have added client-server computing facilities, but those facilities are currently configured to provide gateway access to a mainframe as well as LAN operations and are not marketed separately as a LAN hot site. This author believes that several vendors will begin marketing LAN hot site recovery centers by the time you read this book, there are certain actions and negotiations you can consider to obtain a hot site capability even though they are not currently commercially available.

A *cold* site is a location that can be used to re-establish your LAN operations but which does not currently have any installed data processing equipment. Similar to hot sites which are described in the next section in this chapter, cold sites, too, were first established for data center recovery operations. In fact, cold sites are located mainly in buildings that also house hot sites. In such buildings, one or more large rooms with raised floors and a temperature and humidity controlled environment are used as cold sites.

In the event of a data center disaster, a firm would first relocate its operations to a hot site location. Since a commercial hot site is designed to provide disaster recovery capability for many organizations, the operator of the hot site normally initiates a contractual arrangement with each organization which time limits their use of the hot site. During that period the organization is expected to make arrangements to move their operations either back to their original location or to another location. If the organization's original building has been repaired and equipment replaced prior to the hot site becoming contractually unusable, the organization would move its operations back to the original location. Otherwise, one alternative is to acquire new equipment and move it into the hot site provider's cold site location until a permanent site becomes available.

Alternatives to consider

When moving from a hot site, most organizations will prefer to relocate either back to their original location, if possible, or to a cold site that they can set up by leasing or purchasing an office or building. The reason for this is primarily financial, since operators of hot and cold sites have a substantial overhead which must be amortized during a fraction of the year.

Currently cold sites are set up primarily for data center recovery operations, although there is no reason to preclude an organization from negotiating the use of such cold sites for LAN reconstruction. However, a more practical and perhaps more economical approach is to negotiate with real estate leasing organizations, especially in large metropolitan areas where vacancy rates are currently quite high.

Leasing options for space

Since most LANs do not require any special temperature or humidity controls beyond normal building environment con-

trols, many organizations have been able to obtain prenego-
tiated "cold site" leases for given amounts of office space. Under
those leases, property owners agreed to provide organizations
with immediate office space when needed for a small monthly
fee until the space was required. This type of arrangement was
beneficial to the property owner whose empty office space was
not producing any revenue, as well as to the organization con-
tracting for the space who would pay a much higher fee for
reserving a formal cold site location from a hot site provider.

Intra-company arrangements

If your company has several sites within reasonably close prox-
imity, office space at one location may provide a cold site capability for another location. In considering this option, it is best
to treat negotiations on a formal basis and to develop a memor-
andum of understanding or another type of document that
explicitly describes the use of office space at each location in
the event their use is required. Doing so negates the potential
effect of confusion of responsibilities when personnel relocate,
retire or resign from the company.

Inter-company arrangements

Although not normally considered, inter-company arrangements in which one company agrees to provide temporary office
space to another company during a building disaster represents
a mechanism to acquire a cold site at little to no cost. Of course,
negotiations between companies may be more difficult than
intra-company negotiations and may have to be cleared by their
legal departments. In addition, if the companies are competitive
it may be impractical to attempt to negotiate the potential sharing of office space.

The role of the network bible

The importance of the network bible becomes fully apparent
when a disaster strikes which requires the reconstruction of
your LAN at a cold site. Since that site consists of empty office
space, you must fully reconstruct the LAN. This means you

must order hardware, software and appropriate cabling and communications, install or arrange for its installation, load previously created backup data, configure workstations and servers for operation, and initiate administrative and operational procedures to restore your network to its operational environment prior to the disaster. This could require several weeks or more of effort without the benefit of a network bible, its use can considerably shorten the time required to reconstruct a network.

In fact, in an emergency you can probably obtain most or all of the hardware, software and cable you need to reconstruct your network within a few days or overnight by an express delivery service. However, the primary difficulty organizations face in attempting to reconstruct a network involves ordering and configuring the correct equipment and software and configuring the equipment and software to operate once it's received. Thus, the information in the network bible facilitates both areas and its value is unfortunately recognized most under adverse conditions.

Methods to consider

Two methods you can consider to obtain a hot site capability are intra-company and inter-company negotiations. Concerning intra- company negotiations, you can have two offices of similar size using similar equipment serve as hot-site recovery centers for each other. To head off problems that can occur in the event of a disaster, you should treat intra-company negotiations as if they were occurring with another company and develop an agreement concerning every factor necessary for one office to allow personnel from a second office to use its LAN facilities. This agreement should consider everything from how many employees of one office are temporarily relocated to work in the second office, to their hours of operation, use of equipment, method of gaining access to the building and similar considerations.

Some organizations may have excess workstations that can be connected to the office LAN to enable additional personnel to work at the new office during standard working hours. To do so you must be able to either segment your file servers to allow two sets of LAN applications to co-exist, or integrate the applications of two LANs, both no easy task.

More than likely, personnel from one office will use the equipment from the second office during a different shift. This will provide technical support personnel with the time necessary to take down relevant file servers, substitute removable disks stored at the site which represents the applications and database of the second office, and then bring up the appropriate servers. To do this effectively and efficiently obviously requires a considerable amount of planning.

Hot site agreement elements

To facilitate the planning process, Table 9.1 lists ten specific intra-company hot site agreement elements you may wish to consider.

Declaration of an emergency

In the event of an emergency which destroys or damages the facilities of an office, there should be a procedure to declare the occurrence of an emergency and the use of the hot site. This declaration must occur at the geographic location of the damaged or destroyed site as well as at the recovery or hot site. At the damaged or destroyed site the declaration servers inform key personnel that the emergency situation requires the use of the hot site. That declaration is also used to initiate a notification process to the hot site as well as to inform local personnel that they are temporarily assigned to work at the hot site.

At the hot site the declaration of an emergency is used to

Table 9.1 Intra-company hot site agreement considerations.

Declaration of emergency
Building access
Area access/restrictions
Workstation assignments
Equipment storage/utilization
Server operation/utilization
Work hours/shift assignment
Backup tape storage
Duration of backup site use
Funding

inform key employees that their site will be used as a hot site. This declaration can be used as the starting point for a series of further predefined notifications, such as alerting the building guards that persons on an "emergency list" should be granted a building pass upon arrival and presentation of identification.

Building access

The use of a hot site means some employees from the damaged or destroyed site will require access to the building used as a recovery location. In developing an intra-company hot site agreement, you may wish to consider including the employees that will travel to the recovery site so an access list can be developed ahead of time. In addition, it is a good idea to include the names of key personnel that have authority to modify the access list to reflect changes made necessary by personnel situations or other factors.

Area access controls and restrictions

Since no two offices are exactly alike, there may be areas where transferred employees should not have access. Thus, area access control and restrictions should be predefined.

Workstation assignments

When employees from one office relocate and use the facilities of another office, preplanning the use of workstations can considerably reduce the amount of time required to obtain an effective level of recovery. Thus, preplanning the use of workstations should be considered in an intra-company hot site agreement.

Equipment storage and utilization

Recognizing the disruption to an office caused by additional personnel sharing the use of existing equipment, some organizations may wish to consider acquiring additional equipment for use during emergency operations. If a network is not fully configured to its physical workstation limit, the storage of older PC

Table 9.2 Shift assignment based upon equipment usage.

	Shared server(s)	Dedicated server(s)
Shared workstation	Alternative shift	Alternative shift
Dedicated workstation	Prime shift possible	Prime shift possible

platforms with network adapter cards can provide a solution to the question of what to do with older equipment as well as facilitate recovery operations when such operations become necessary. For example, the replacement of 80386 PCs with 80486 computers could result in the storage of the older 80386 based computers for use in an emergency.

Another area of concern with respect to equipment storage involves situations where the hot site does not have appropriate equipment to provide a desired level of recovery. One organizational entity can then consider funding the acquisition of equipment to be located at the hot site to facilitate recovery operations. Both the funding and utilization of equipment should be considered in the intra-company hot site agreement.

Server operation and utilization

As previously discussed, you can consider the shared use of existing servers or separate shifts during which existing servers are reconfigured for use. Another alternative you can consider is the use of separate dedicated servers to support the recovery operations of the personnel relocated to the hot site. The effect of shared and dedicated workstations and servers upon shift operations is examined next.

Work hours and shift assignments

To minimize disruption resulting from personnel from one office using the facilities of another office, you should consider defining the work hours and any necessary shift assignments required for recovery operations. Shift assignments will primarily be based upon how equipment is used at the hot site— shared or dedicated use. Table 9.2 indicates when you can consider prime shift operations in comparison with the use of alternative shift operations based upon the use of shared and dedicated equipment.

Backup tape storage

The use of another company office as a hot site also makes that office a viable candidate to store backup tapes. If LANs in each office covered by an intra-company hot site agreement are connected by leased line communications facilities, it may be possible to use those facilities after normal business hours to televault updates between sites. Otherwise, you can consider the use of the switched telephone network for televaulting. The use of office storage facilities, frequency of tape transmission, and equipment required for televaulting operations should be incorporated into the intra-company hot site agreement.

Duration of backup site use

No matter how carefully planned, the use of equipment and facilities in one office by personnel from another office will be disruptive to the operations of both the relocated and hot site office. Although you do not want to evict other personnel from the use of your facilities during a recovery operation, there should be a fixed duration to the use of a hot site. That duration should be based upon a reasonable estimate of the maximum amount of time to acquire new office facilities and install required cabling and equipment to resume operations.

Funding

The use of a pair of corporate offices as effective hot site facilities to backup one another will more than likely require the installation of additional equipment at each site. Thus, the funding, ownership, testing and use of such equipment prior to and during a recovery operation should be considered in an intra-company hot site agreement.

Inter-company hot site agreements

In comparison with an intra-company agreement, an inter-company agreement may be much more difficult to negotiate. Although both agreements will more than likely include elements similar to those listed in Table 9.1, inter-company agreements may require approval at the highest operational levels. In addition, regardless of the merits of one company office serving as a backup site for another company, if both organizations are in competitive industries or businesses it may be politically difficult to obtain approval for any agreement to share computer and office resources.

Final words

The probability of occurrence of a real disaster which destroys some or all of an organization's client-server equipment is relatively small, perhaps less than your chance of being mugged while touring Washington, D.C. However, if disaster strikes, it is most important to have contingency plans, including the ability to operate equipment at an alternative location until your location is reconstructed or the use of a new office and the installation of new equipment permits your employees to resume operations. To paraphrase the Boy Scout motto, "Proper planning provides organizations with the ability to survive".

INDEX

LOCAL AREA NETWORKING

PROTECTING LAN RESOURCES
A Comprehensive Guide to Securing, Protecting and Rebuilding a Network

With the evolution of distributed computing, security is now a key issue for network users. This comprehensive guide will provide network managers and users with a detailed knowledge of the techniques and tools they can use to secure their data against unauthorised users. Gil Held also provides guidance on how to prevent disasters such as self-corruption of data and computer viruses.
1995   0 471 95407 1

LAN PERFORMANCE
Issues and Answers

The performance of LANs depends upon a large number of variables, including the access method, the media and cable length, the bridging and the gateway methods. This text covers all these variables to enable the reader to select and design equipment for reliability and high performance.
1994   0 471 94223 5

TOKEN- RING NETWORKS
Characteristics, Operation, Construction and Management

This timely book provides the reader with a comprehensive understanding of how Token-Ring networks operate, the constraints and performance issues that affect their implementation, and how their growth and use can be managed both locally and as part of an Enterprise network.
1993 0 471 94041 0

ETHERNET NETWORKS
Design, Implementation, Operation, and Management

1994 0 471 59717 1

REFERENCE

DICTIONARY OF COMMUNICATIONS TECHNOLOGY
Terms, Definitions and Abbreviations

1995 0 471 95126 9 (Paper)
         0 471 95542 6 (Cloth)

THE COMPLETE MODEM REFERENCE
2nd Edition

1994 0 471 00852 4

THE COMPLETE PC AT AND COMPATIBLES REFERENCE MANUAL

1991 0 471 53315 7